SCENES FROM THE PAST: 11

RAILWAYS IN AND AR...

NOTTINGHAM

London Road Junction, c.1952. It is impossible within the confines of this book to illustrate every type of locomotive which came to the city, and although the distinctive Beyer-Garratts gathered in large numbers only a few miles down the line at Toton, they were by no means an everyday sight in Nottingham. However, this work would not be complete without an illustration of one of these machines, which were rather awkward to photograph. The raised camera position adopted enables the entire length of the engine to be caught without the result looking somewhat contrived. No. 47987 has, unusually, avoided the goods lines and drawn its train through the platform roads.

by

VIC FORSTER & BILL TAYLOR

Designed and edited by Gregory K. Fox
Typeset by Ryburn Typesetting, Halifax
Printed by The Amadeus Press, Huddersfield

Published by Foxline Publishing
32 Urwick Road, Romiley, Stockport SK6 3JS

POSTSCRIPT

It is with sadness that the death of Vic Forster in February 1991 is reported. Vic, long time resident of Beeston, elder statesman of the Railway Correspondence and Travel Society, and admirer of the steam railway age, was mentioned by way of acknowledgment time and again in books dealing with his favourite subject, but until now his name has not appeared on the title page. How regrettable that a longstanding illness should claim his life before he could see the fruits of his labours.

Nottingham Midland, c.1949. It's still quite soon after nationalisation and an LMS Compound No. 41057, with the name of its new owner spelled out in full on the tender, stands at platform 4 under the bridge carrying the rival line into the city, ready to take a Derby train out. It couldn't be anywhere else but Nottingham Midland.
Photo: J.F. Henton

ACKNOWLEDGMENTS

Starting out with an idea and a handful of pictures and transforming them into this publication has been an enjoyable task, but impossible to accomplish unaided. We must therefore give three acknowledgments as follows.

In preparing the text we have made reference to previously published material including ordnance survey maps, both public and working timetables, and books, in particular the Regional History of the Railways of Great Britain Volume 9, and the R.C.T.S. series on LNER locomotives; in addition Grinling's History of the Great Northern Railway and the pamphlet concerning Nottingham's Railways by the Railway and Canal Historical Society have been consulted. Whilst great care has been taken to avoid them, any mistakes are the responsibility of the authors alone.

Secondly a few words about the photographs, the majority of which are culled from the authors' collections, but principally that of Vic Forster. Where the photographer's identity is known due acknowledgment has been given, but a substantial number of prints in Vic's enormous library do not reveal such information and can only be attributed to his collection. Were it not for the combined work of these camera artists, executed individually from about 1920 onwards, we would not be writing these few lines to express our grateful thanks to them, one and all, for their past deeds, because this glimpse into Nottingham's byegone years could never have been revealed.

Finally our thanks go to Gregory Fox for assisting with illustrations, for dealing with the layout and design, for over two years of patient encouragement given to us, not least for introducing a series of books, factual yet nostalgic, which have proved appealing to a wider public than the railway buff alone, and finally for having the conviction to warrant our effort worthy of inclusion in the Scenes from the Past series.

INTRODUCTION

It is a remarkable thing that a comparison between the present day railway system serving Nottingham as depicted on the map inside the back cover of this book with the situation as it existed in 1850 reveals an almost identical position obtaining in geographical terms at dates one hundred and forty years apart, for in 1850 the then Midland Station was to be found on a through route from Derby to Lincoln to which was connected a branch line running through the northern suburbs of Basford and Bulwell proceeding up the valley of the River Leen and ultimately reaching Mansfield. All these lines were owned by the Midland Railway Company which had been formed in 1844 as a sensible merger between three early companies whose main lines radiated from Derby. A few miles to the east of the city, at Netherfield, a connection went off in a south-easterly direction crossing the River Trent near Radcliffe and joining what is now the East Coast Main Line from Kings Cross to Edinburgh at Grantham. This line was independently promoted and built, and, had the MR been successful in absorbing it when it tried, the history and development of the railways around Nottingham would have been a very different story.

Rails of sorts were laid as early as 1604 enabling coal mined at Strelley to be taken down to the Trent, but this was merely one of several similar tramroads constructed in the 17th and 18th centuries to carry coal, sand, and other minerals to the navigable rivers and later to join up with the canal network. However, it was not until the coming of the Midland Counties Railway, whose origins can be traced back to a meeting of Erewash Valley coal owners at the Sun Inn, Eastwood, on 16 August 1832 (which place incidentally therefore claims to be the birthplace of the MR) that the system of lines discussed and illustrated in this book emerges.

Having obtained parliamentary authority for its construction in 1836 the MCR took a little over two years to build the first section of its line which connected Nottingham with Derby, and with much ceremony, as befitted the occasion, the first special trains ran on 30th May 1839. A few days later, on the 4 June, the terminal station at Carrington Street witnessed the departure of the 7am train to Derby and thus made Nottingham part of the railway age. The city was given rail access to London from the 30th June 1840 although for the ensuing 22 years passengers had first to travel to Derby before retracing their route as far as Trent before proceeding via Leicester and Rugby, where a junction was effected with the London and Birmingham Railway. Then, following formation of the MR in 1844, an event which fortunately preceded the Railway Mania of the following year, some expansion took place with the branch to Lincoln being opened on 4 August 1846, followed on the 2nd October 1848 by the Leen Valley line as far as Kirkby-in-Ashfield. The former branch left the MCR a short distance to the west of Carrington Street Station rather than, as might have been expected, by an end on junction. However, the cumbersome arrangement of having to reverse Lincoln bound trains out of the station before setting off in an easterly direction was overcome when the new MR station was brought into use on the 22nd May 1848, these premises having a pleasing, if not ornate frontage to the newly named Station Street. The MR can therefore be regarded as the local company which, following expansion, became the established railway serving the city, then and as it does today as part of BR. When this country's railways were nationalised in 1948, the MR had for the preceding 25 years been a part of the London Midland and Scottish Railway.

Its position in the city remained strong for many years, enjoying what was a near monopoly until the mid 1870's when significant new construction by the Great Northern Railway, intended primarily to tap the developing Nottinghamshire and Derbyshire coalfield, came about, and was responded to by the MR with its construction of the short connecting line between Radford on the Mansfield branch and Trowell on the Erewash Valley main line, thus affording more direct access to Sheffield and beyond than did the wayward route via Long Eaton. This line, opened on 1st May 1875, when used in conjunction with the Nottingham to Melton Mowbray line (opened for passengers on 4th February 1880) gave the MR the opportunity to place Nottingham for the first time on a through main line route, allowing express trains to pause at the Midland Station on their way from St. Pancras to Bradford or Glasgow.

In stark contrast, the GNR might well be referred to as the invader. It gained a foothold in the district by taking a long lease of the grandly styled Ambergate, Nottingham & Boston & Eastern Junction Railway, which built the line from Netherfield to Grantham already referred to. For this advantage it had to thank one of its shareholders, Graham Hutchinson, for seeing off the MR challenge to take over the line in 1851. The AN&B&EJR realised its strategic importance, lying as it did between the Hudson controlled MR empire in the west and the East Coast main line,

i) Nottingham Midland, 15th June 1903. This view east along Station Street shows the 1848 entrance that was brought into use soon after the opening of the line to Lincoln. —*Photo: Author's collection*

ii) London Road Low Level. This is the best view of Low Level Station taken looking along the approach road, the view being from the Northwest. Although an attractive building, this Great Northern station contained a mixture of architectural variations. Its *porte cochère* – large porch to allow vehicles access – was arguably its main feature. Gordon Biddle in his book *Victorian Stations*, describes the station. "Asymmetrical and partly curved, it combined a Frenchified gable and turret; square, round-headed and Venetian windows; a highly original 'T' shaped *porte cochère*; and Tudor-inspired diamond-patterned parapets interspersed with stone balustrading." Passenger trains stopped calling from 22nd May 1944 but public service, in the form of goods traffic, continued until December 1972.

and it was therefore well placed to secure a good deal for its shareholders. The same Hutchinson persuaded the GNR of the benefits to be gained by having this line under its control playing a large part in bringing together the two companies who were parties to the lease.

The Ambergate Company as it was known operated from 15th July 1850 to a junction with the MR at Netherfield, but soon built its own line to the city from that point and on 3rd October 1857 brought into use its terminus at London Road (later to be called London Road Low Level) no more than a couple of hundred yards away from the rival MR establishment on Station Street. The underlying reason for this section of line being built can be found in the various conflicts which arose between the MR and the AN&B&EJR, conflicts of which the GNR was well aware. Difficulties encountered with the MR relating to the carriage of Derbyshire coal, which the MR regarded as its own, eventually drove the GNR to use the line which it had leased as a springboard for an extensive development of new lines around the northern perimeter of the city continuing westwards to Derby and beyond and which lines crossed the southern ends of the Erewash and Leen valleys where the coal was being brought to the surface. Naturally enough, the GNR built a line from Giltbrook, near Kimberley, along the Erewash Valley as far as Pinxton, which saw its first passenger trains on 1 August 1876, and one from a point east of Basford close by the present day City Hospital to Newstead opened on 1st October 1882 and commencing at the appropriately named Leen Valley Junction. That same jealousy with which the MR had guarded its business from the pits now worked against it, for the coalowners welcomed the competition in transport costs which came with the arrival of the "Derbyshire Lines" as these GNR extensions were called.

Nor had the GNR finished yet, for it spread its tentacles beyond the coalfield to reach the breweries of Burton-on-Trent and out as far as the rich pasture land east of Stafford from which district it secured a valuable traffic in milk for London. Much land was available at Colwick, east of Nottingham, and this persuaded the GNR to establish sidings and a locomotive shed here, a facility which eventually blossomed forth to become a main shed in LNER days housing well over 200 engines, many of which could be seen in the adjacent sprawling mass of Colwick Yards. All this originated in 1878, and on the 1st July of that year a line from Bottesford West Junction on the Grantham line, to Newark, was opened, followed about twelve months later by the Great Northern and London & North Western Joint line but of which more later.

By 1882 the GNR could content itself that it was carrying a reasonable share of the remunerative coal traffic, but its position as to passenger services was not so good. Arguably the London Road Terminus was no less conveniently sited in relation to the city than the MR station, but local passengers to the outer suburbs of Daybrook, Basford and Bulwell to say nothing of the industrial towns then rapidly expanding further afield, examples being Ilkeston, Eastwood, Pinxton, Hucknall and Kirkby-in-Ashfield, were obliged to go by a circuitous route via Netherfield, a most indirect journey involving an eastwards trek for the first three miles before turning eventually through 180 degrees and using the overcrowded and steeply graded line past Gedling to Daybrook. Partly in order to overcome this problem, and partly to serve the expanding residential quarters in the hilly area north east of the city a local line was promoted called the Nottingham Suburban Railway, opening on the 2nd December 1889 and being worked from the outset by the GNR. The new line left the Grantham route at Trent Lane East Junction, turning sharply northwards, and connecting with the earlier GNR lines just to the east of Daybrook Station, and although having some very stiff gradients, it gave three districts near the city a railway station for the first time, and in the process saved about 3½ miles as compared with the Gedling detour, thus benefitting the local services to the mining valleys and out to Derby. Except for the closure of the MR station at Lenton the NSR stations were destined to be the first in the area to lose their service. The later development of the GNR concerning Nottingham is bound up with the arrival of the fourth and last company to serve the city, but before this, mention must be made of the London & North Western Railway which arrived on the scene courtesy of running powers granted by the GNR from Saxondale Junction, east of Radcliffe-on-Trent, to London Road Station.

The GNR and LNWR had combined to build what was called, not surprisingly, the Joint Line, through east Leicestershire with the idea of establishing a through rail link between Northampton and Newark. Opened on 1st September 1879, this enabled Northampton the following year to have a through train to Nottingham (and vice versa) for the first time, but more importantly for the LNWR it gave that company a sound and valuable connection with the Derbyshire and Nottinghamshire coalfield, by means of further running powers which it exercised over those portions of the GNR "Derbyshire Lines" serving the pits. A commodious goods warehouse was provided by the LNWR at Manvers Street by means of a short east facing branch on the north side of the Grantham line near to

Trent Lane Junctions. More substantially the same company built an eight road locomotive shed out at Colwick, together with workmen's dwellings appropriately called *London & North Western Terrace*. Such was the extent of the coal traffic carried by the LNWR over the GNR lines that further sidings were laid at Colwick to accommodate the extra trains. As can be seen, very little track mileage was provided by the company but it nevertheless secured an excellent footing in Nottingham by means of a policy whereby it opposed the construction of new lines, subsequently supporting them in exchange for running powers and in the process saving itself much capital outlay. To the LNWR, Nottingham was an enclave.

Of all the railway companies which existed before the first world war the Great Central Railway was the fourth and last to come to the city. Formerly a provincial company calling itself the Manchester Sheffield & Lincolnshire Railway, it made plans in the early 1890s to build lines which would ultimately enable it to reach London and on 15th March 1899 the public service commenced from Marylebone to Sheffield and Manchester taking in Nottingham on the way. Much has already been written, and doubtless more will follow as to whether or not the line should have been built and when its closure became evident in the 1960s further arguments arose, still ongoing, as to the wisdom or otherwise of its demise. So far as relates to Nottingham, the clock tower which rose above the joint station of the GCR and GNR stands today as a permanent reminder that come it did, and not without style.

Running in a nearly straight line free from sharp curves to hinder its expresses, the GCR bisected the lace city from north to south, striding magnificently across the Leen Valley at Bulwell over a long blue brick viaduct, was then carried over a substantial embankment on the approach to New Basford soon after passing the site of new connections forged with the GNR, plunging into the depths of Sherwood Rise and Mansfield Road tunnels to emerge at Victoria Station; next digging its way out under Thurland Street before crossing at rooftop level on a succession of bridges and viaducts everything which stood in its path, including the Midland Station, and finally leaving the city behind on a four tracked girder bridge which spanned the River Trent. It is said that the station derived its name at the suggestion of the Lord Mayor of Nottingham because the two owning companies could not settle upon a name, so Victoria was put forward as the station opened on the Queen's birthday, the 24th May 1900. The new station was certainly closer to the market and other shops and offices than was the Midland Station, at that time still located on Station Street, and as well as enabling the GNR, at last, to have a direct route for its local passenger services, it truly placed Nottingham on a main line railway and gave passengers, in many cases for the first time, the opportunity to reach distant places without having to change trains.

The advantages in the siting of Victoria Station secured by its rivals prompted the MR to put in hand a rebuilding of its own premises, carried out in 1903/4 when, amongst other improvements, the present day entrance, booking hall and other facilities fronting to Carrington Street were added. The GCR made its impression on the city in the form of a main line.

At the maximum development of lines of railway the city was lavishly provided for, but alas, most of what existed has disappeared. There remain in Nottingham two railway built clock towers, but only the Midland's slightly younger one stands within the sound of trains, which brings us back to the map referred to in the opening paragraph. A quick glance at this makes us realise just how much has gone, and from there, it is but a short step to reflect on times past and recall the local railway scene of 20, 40 or maybe 60 years ago. Those born too late to have personal memories are less fortunate, and have to imagine what Nottingham's railways were like in times past. The journey through the pages of this book takes young and old alike to most of the relevant places in and around the city, and we are well rewarded it that journey gives pleasure.

iii) Nottingham Victoria, c.1930. The frontage to Mansfield Road showing the covered taxi rank in the forecourt, also part of the Victoria Hotel. On the wall by the pedestrian entrance to the booking hall day trips to Bradford and York are advertised at 25/– (for the benefit of those of us who are not predecimal £1.25). It is probably worth noting that the station was now halfway through its period of existence. Perhaps more pertinent however is the fact that it is almost three decades since its demise!

1. Attenborough, c.1917. This photograph takes us back to the pre-grouping era at Attenborough. Although the train hides the station buildings, only the chimney above the waiting room being clearly visible, nevertheless the photograph has its own particular story to tell. Attenborough was a small village close by the River Trent when the station was built and at that time had no strong connections with industry. It was discovered that this area was rich in gravel deposits which led over a period of time to the establishment and development of a considerable business with excavations being made particularly in a narrow ribbon of land lying between the river and the line of railway. In turn the gravel pits have themselves been filled in and are stocked with fish providing a venue for the locals to relax in a traditional manner. The other development came with the establishment at Chilwell, just to the west of Attenborough Station, of the military depot which was immediately connected to the line of the MR by a junction on the north side between Attenborough and Trent. This munitions factory was in full production during the first world war and employed large numbers of people whose homes were far enough away to warrant the running of special trains. In order to cope with the volume of workers many of these work people's trains comprised more coaches than the expresses of the day, but nevertheless were worked by the charming four coupled tank engines built at Derby. As evidenced by this illustration the vehicles were mostly six wheeled and here MR No. 1409 with no less than 13 vehicles in tow, stands on the eastbound track ready to leave. It was quickly discovered that the original station platforms, though perfectly adequate for every day use could not cope with these work people's trains which were obliged to draw forward at least once, a situation which could not be tolerated at a time of national emergency with a result that both up and down platforms were lengthened to meet the situation. No doubt the MR Company would not have to bear the entire cost of this new work but certainly Attenborough retained this unusual feature for a very long time.

2. Attenborough, c.1914–18. The existence of an inordinately long section of fence here did not go unnoticed by contemporary manufacturers who paid the railway company a small annual fee for the privilege of allowing their wares to be advertised. Perhaps a lot of dirty folk lived in Attenborough for about half of the vitreous enamel signs, long since disappeared from ordinary view but nostalgically displayed at Britain's preserved railway centres, advertise soap. Curious to say, when television advertising was unleashed upon us there was a surfeit of commercials relating to Daz, Omo and the like. Does anyone remember Surf and Mrs. Bradshaw?

The chimneyed building is the older of the two on the Nottingham bound platform, parts of it may well date back to when the station was opened but it does appear that some modification has been carried out with a generous provision of windows on the platform elevation. When the station was opened the platforms were considerably shorter than appears in this illustration and were at that time of sufficient length to accommodate the local passenger trains seeking business here. The further of the two buildings did not appear until around the time of the first world war, its purpose being to cater for the several hundreds of workers at the nearby Chilwell Ordnance Depot who made daily use of this station.

3. Chilwell, n.d. A short distance to the west of Attenborough Station a line went off to serve the once extensive war department railway system of the Chilwell Ordnance Depot. A small stud of shunting engines was kept for work in the sidings in later years these usually being the familiar war department saddle tanks which were kept busy particularly at times of national emergency. The second world war is an obvious example but later than this came the Suez crisis which produced a heavy volume of traffic both to and from this location. During the first world war several workers trains were operated to nearby Attenborough Station for the benefit of civilian workers engaged by the military, and one supposes that the sidings were filled with rolling stock of both military and railway company origin but it was impossible to operate so many work peoples services into the depot itself. This however was a practice developed in later years, the last train using the depot as a terminus will be the long standing Mansfield service not advertised in the public timetable. The train usually composed of four coaches took the west curve at Lenton and thereby not only avoided Nottingham but gave its patrons the opportunity to travel on two sections of line not normally used for passenger services, the second one of course being the line into the depot itself. Mansfield shed kept one small tender engine for many years purposely to fulfil this duty, No. 46501 having the virtual monopoly until transferred away to be replaced by the locomotive seen in this view No. 78020. The late afternoon return working to Mansfield appears ready to go, sizzling at the safety valves whilst the man in the foreground will walk ahead of the train as far as the place where the Ministry of Defence line joins the BR branch. The distinct lack of signals of any type will be noticed as also the gauntleted track to the right of the picture which forms the weighbridge the adjacent cabin being responsible for weighing and documenting everything which left the depot by rail.

Photo: W. Reed

4. Beeston, pre 1923. A developing residential area on the fringe of a city blessed with manufacturing industries in an era when the motor car had not yet established itself persuaded the MR to improve the original passenger facilities here. More shelter for those passengers using the frequent service together with cheap workmen's and season tickets drew a large patronage to the line which was obviously noticed by the contemporary advertising executives who had a field day. Beeston is fortunate in that it has always enjoyed a good train service, a state of affairs which seems set to continue. Furthermore, on those occasions when R.C.T.S. East Midlander specials have set sail or returned along this line, they always seem to have had a scheduled stop at Beeston. I wonder why?

5. Beeston, June 1956. Dating from the middle of the last century and seemingly destined to survive for the foreseeable future due to its status as a listed building, the MR Buildings dating from 1847 graced the Nottingham bound platform. No corrugated metal or rotting timber in this illustration but a pleasant glass canopy overhead with gables projecting outwards from the masonry serves to divert rainwater into gullies. An attentive employee seems to be implying that the barrows are loaded and all is ready for the arrival of the next train. Within the last few years this building has had further maintenance work carried out, timely for the Midland Counties Railway 150 celebrations in 1989.   *Photo: J.F. Henton*

6. Beeston, c.1953. Everything seems to be competing for the available space in this busy episode looking east from the station footbridge. The level crossing gates swung to and fro more than a hundred times a day to give precedence first to road and then to railway. Indeed both were very busy with immediate tail backs of traffic building up the moment the gates closed and at times even the trains were queuing up to get through this double track bottle neck. For once the signalman gets 2 trains on their way with only one closing of the gates, a very mixed goods train making its way towards Nottingham whilst 2-6-4 tank No. 42636 has charge of a local to Derby. The thoughtful placing of the footbridge at least gave pedestrians the opportunity to avoid delay.
                Photo: J.J. Foreman

7. Carlton and Netherfield, c.1958. The traffic on the main street in Carlton was interrupted many times each day by the opening and closing of the level crossing gates. As road traffic increased the problem became acute but the crossing remains in operation to this day although the congestion has been alleviated to some extent by keeping cars away from the main street.

Most of the traffic comprised stopping passenger trains between Nottingham and Lincoln together with mineral trains and returning empties to and from Staythorpe Power Station near Newark. Four coaches on this Nottingham to Lincoln train headed by Fowler 2-6-4 tank number 42339 just nicely fit into the platform where a staggered arrangement exists, the up platform beyond the level crossing gates incorporating the main station buildings and booking office.   *Photo: C.A. Hill*

NOTTINGHAM MIDLAND

8. Nottingham Midland, 5th February 1930. The impressive Carrington Street entrance to the station, completed in 1904, provided the perfect answer to the Great Central Company, whose Victoria Station had opened some four years previously. The front of the building was in effect a façade fronting the covered cab approach, features similar to that found at Leicester London Road. The orange brown terracotta, so favoured by the Midland, has been restored in recent years to full advantage. *Photo: National Railway Museum*

Nottingham Midland Station

Speaking shortly after the passing of the Midland Counties Railway Bill in 1836 when it became apparent that Nottingham would be at the end of a branch line, one member of the City Corporation regretting the fact that his fellow citizens had shown a lack of enthusiasm for the new mode of transport, commented significantly that Nottingham ought to have found itself placed on a through north to south line of railway and that the neighbouring town of Derby had secured for itself that particular advantage. When uttering those words of wisdom he could hardly have been expected to foresee that 150 years or so later a similar situation would prevail in that Derby would enjoy a range of Inter-City services not only to the capital but also to the North East and Scotland as well as to the South Western quarter of Britain via Birmingham, whilst Nottingham to all intents and purposes would again be at the end of the same branch line causing the St. Pancras to Sheffield trains to deviate from the direct line and to make a reversal in Nottingham Station.

So it was that the city's first railway station was a terminus whose façade stood almost directly opposite the present day entrance to Nottingham Station on what is now Carrington Street. The station buildings however were located at track level and at the time of building fronted to no existing highway and hence a road had to be formed from the city to the station in order to attract travellers. Two platform faces were provided with four lines of rail separating them and it is clear from early illustrations they had been built of stone, the façade at the eastern end being two storey whilst the platform buildings were symmetrical, the passengers being protected by a cast iron pitched roof which spanned the platform and the first running line in each case. The middle two lines were covered by a third roof of similar construction and profile but only extending for about half platform length at the eastern end.

On the 4th December 1843 Queen Victoria no less travelled by train from Chesterfield to Nottingham en route to Belvoir Castle and after being received by the Lord Mayor and other worthies Her Majesty continued the journey by carriage along the new road which had been formed parallel to the line of railway but to the south east and which to this day is known as Queen's Road.

On 3rd August 1846 the extension to Lincoln was opened but the junction was located west of the station which for a while meant that any train calling at Nottingham had to reverse out of the terminus beyond the junction, said to have been 26 chains west of the station, in order to gain access to the Lincoln line, the route of which passed just to the south thereof. This clumsy arrangement caused inconvenience not just for the railway who soon eased the burden temporarily by the provision of a further platform line along the southern elevation of the station, thus enabling trains to run through to Lincoln without reversal, but additionally for users of Queen's Road who now had to contend with what amounted to two level crossing cheek by jowl. The MR Company quickly saw the wisdom of providing better facilities for through running and made plans for an entire new station east of the original one this time with a long frontage parallel with and to the north of the running lines on a new street, appropriately enough called Station Street.

On 22nd May 1848 the new premises were brought into use, the station site covering an area about 600 feet long by 94 feet wide, the station buildings having a frontage measuring 180 feet and incorporating a projecting stone portico some 50 feet long by 12 feet high. From the same date the original station closed for business but was later used as goods offices for some years until new and more commodious goods offices were provided on the same site at which time the original station was demolished with the exception of the stone pillars marking the entrance gateway and these survive even now.

If the new station constituted a great improvement to patrons of the railway it did nothing whatsoever to improve the lot of the unfortunate road user who wished to travel south out of the city, for no matter whether he chose London Road, Queen's Road or Wilford Road, he had to cross the railway line on the level. The city fathers had seen these problems for many

continued over

years and a committee of enquiry had been appointed as long ago as 1848. Its efforts went unrewarded until 1861 during which year an agreement was made with the MR Company that a bridge would be provided over the railway line at Wilford Road the work being completed two years later. Queen's Road, however, was more difficult because the provision of a bridge here over the two level crossings also necessitated the road level at the northern approach being raised to such an extent that it interfered with other buildings including what is now the Bentinck Hotel. At the end of 1869 Queen's Road at last passed above the railway line and at the same time the opportunity was taken to provide a third passenger platform and to the south of that, separate goods lines, because the West Croft Canal was no longer used and had been filled in. So by the beginning of the 1870's the

continued below

to the east of the 1869 road overbridge already mentioned, which by now was called Carrington Street and was established as a main thoroughfare running right to the heart of the city. The Midland therefore embarked upon a substantial development in the rectangle of land enclosed by the GC line, Queen's Road (as it now is), Carrington Street and Station Street and by extending the platform in a westerly direction and building a new entrance from Carrington Street complete with booking facilities, taxi rank from which the platforms could be reached by means of staircases, the MR provided Nottingham with a station worthy of any city emulating Victoria Station even as far as being crowned by the mandatory Clock Tower.

As with the building of Victoria Station this virtual re-building by the MR in 1903 and 1904 has been well photographed, some of these

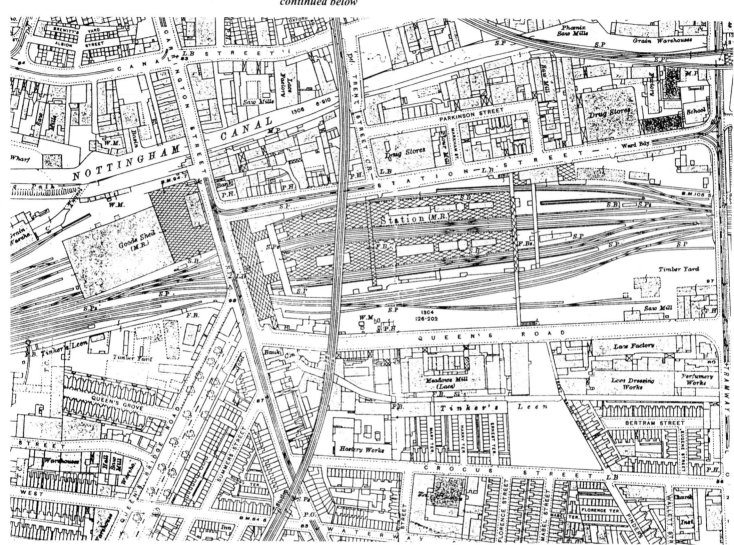

MR had made its peace with the Nottingham Corporation and was now looking forward to the surge of expansion over the following ten years which, using the Radford–Trowell cut off of 1875 and the Melton Mowbray line of 1880, put Nottingham on a through line from London to the north of England, and indeed beyond, for from February 1882 the forerunners of the Thames Clyde Express paused on their lengthy journey.

The last quarter of the nineteenth century saw more industrial growth particularly with the expansion of the coalfield lying to the north of the city and with it came more housing to cope with noticeable increase in population all of which was bound sooner or later to break the near monopoly of the MR. It came sooner in fact with the new lines developed by the GNR from the 1870's and just when everyone thought that the railway map of the city was complete a new competitor for coal and passenger traffic entered the scene in the shape of the impudent GCR with its main line to London.

Towards the end of Queen Victoria's reign the industrial hustle and bustle of the city had edged away from the Midland Railway Station so that by the time the GCR arrived on the scene with its magnificent new station built jointly with the GNR the MR felt bound to improve its own facilities once more. The new line of the GCR swept majestically at right angles high over the western platform ends of the Midland Station a short distance

illustrations appearing in this book. The Nottingham Midland Station which was re-opened on 17th January 1904 is in almost every detail the premises used by BR today and happily the exterior masonry has in recent years undergone a complete cleaning process which, especially when sunlit, gives the station a most pleasing appearance and a welcome relief from the undercoated rectangular buildings created by post war architectural thinking.

In its final form the operational part of the station comprised six platforms running almost exactly east to west, and which, with the exception of platform 6, comprised effectively two large islands. The northerly one was flanked by platform 1 which was nearest to Station Street and which was used almost exclusively for trains departing eastwards or along the Melton line. Platform 2 was indented into the eastern end of the island adjacent to Nottingham East Signal Box whilst platform 3 ran along the south face and could be used for express trains departing in either direction, the layout controlled by Nottingham West Signal Box being such as to permit trains to Derby, Leicester or Chesterfield to leave platform 3. All the usual passenger facilities could be found on this platform including waiting rooms of generous proportions which were warmed by coal fires when occasion required, toilet facilities, luggage lift, platform seats, book stall contracted out to W.H. Smith,

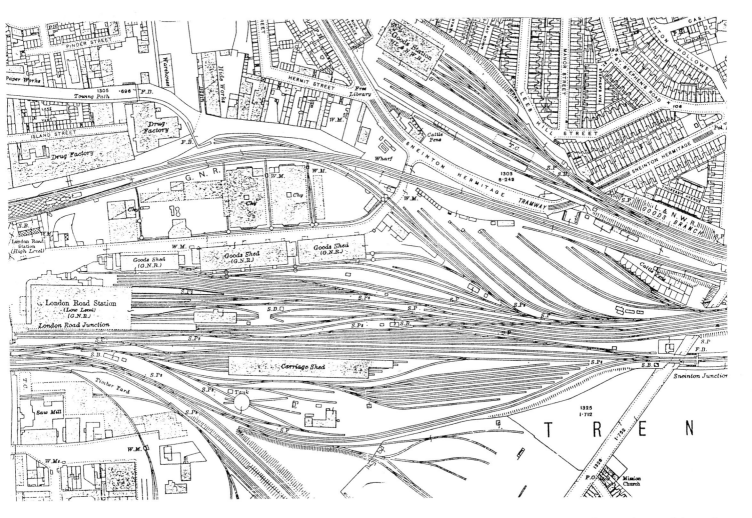

telephones, chocolate dispensing machines and the particularly ornate refreshment room which was rather overdone with houseplants. From the moment the traveller left Carrington Street he was protected from the elements and was sheltered from the rain at all times for although the station was not provided with an overall roof, each of the main island platforms had a canopy running from the foot of the stairs for most of the length of the platform comprising a succession of wrought iron gables extending outwards to the platform edge and fringed by the decorative fret work so typical of railway architecture.

Between platforms 3 and 4 lay four running lines for most of the length although at each end the number was reduced to three.

Of the two non platform lines the more northerly one was designated "middle loop" and could be used for through running in either direction. The other line was more often than not used as a siding to stable coaching stock not immediately required. About midway along the length of the platforms crossover points were provided controlled by Station B Box which was on the platform. A little way to the east of the GC overbridge a pedestrian footbridge with double staircases facing both east and west gave ample pedestrian connection between the two main island platforms and indeed the footbridge was continued in a southerly direction to connect with platform 6. This second island was flanked by platforms 4 and 5 respectively on the north and south sides thereof, and although both of these platforms were useable either way the pattern of service was such that they were used almost exclusively for westbound departures. The passenger facilities here matched those on platforms 1 and 3 and were arguably better patronised, for the great majority of long distance trains, for example to Bradford, Glasgow, Manchester and St. Pancras (via Leicester) made use of platforms 5 and 4 which seems to give the impression that they were being overworked in comparison with the rest of the station. Platform 6 which was separated from number 5 by three running lines was very definitely with poor relation being devoid of nearly all the passenger comforts previously described. Protection from the elements was very limited and the waiting passengers were very lucky if they could find a seat to rest their weary bodies. The operation of the platform was again bi-directional and in fairness to the authorities it should be said that few timetabled trains even used platform 6, it being reserved for the most part for special trains and excursion traffic such as the rail tours organised by the East Midlands branch of the Railway Correspondence and Travel Society. In bygone years

separate goods lines looped around the southern perimeter of the station complex, their workings being controlled directly between the signal boxes at Wilford Road and London Road junction and it was uncommon for any non-passenger traffic to pass through the station lines. However as far as the passenger traffic was concerned there were four intermediate signal boxes between the two just named of which Station East on account of its position was far and away the most photographed. Only 249 yards separated that Box from London Road junction and 473 yards was the distance between it and Station West Signal Box which was located just beyond Carrington Street road bridge. Small signal boxes were provided on each of the main island platforms referred to as Station B and Station A, the latter being the only one of the signal boxes in the vicinity of Midland Station not to be open continuously according to official records in 1959.

It must not be supposed that London trains always ran into St. Pancras for that great station was not opened until the year 1868. The Midland Railway, unlike most of the other northern lines, developed to rather than from the capital which meant that the earliest route was by way of Leicester and Rugby where the London and Birmingham railway was joined for the 82 mile run into Euston. Later the MR forged southwards from Leicester by way of Bedford to Hitchin where a junction was effected with the main line of its old rival the GNR and by means of running powers it reached Kings Cross; mileage on foreign tracks was substantially reduced. With the opening of St. Pancras it was possible at last to entrain at Midland Station and remain on the tracks of one company for the entire journey via Leicester.

The year 1876 saw the opening of the famed Settle and Carlisle line which brought the MR into the reckoning as a carrier of Anglo-Scottish traffic and with the completion of the Melton line in 1882, some of the Scotch Expresses were diverted to serve Nottingham. The number of daily passenger trains calling at or starting from the Midland Station probably peaked about 1914 when railways were competing fiercely with electric trams on routes close to city centres (hence the closure of Lenton Station) but before the motor car was owned by other than the well-heeled. At the zenith local trains usually calling at all intermediate stations ran on the routes to Newark and Lincoln; to Melton Mowbray and some going through to Kettering whilst others got no further than Widmerpool; Leicester; Castle Donnington via Sheet Stores Junction; the Derby line with the occasional train progressing to Ambergate and in later years to Matlock and even

continued over

9. Nottingham Midland, 11th September 1903. The extent of the improvements are fast becoming evident in this view of the Cab Approach from the Queens Road end looking north.

Bakewell; up the Erewash Valley to Chesterfield and Sheffield usually via Long Eaton but sometimes using the Radford-Trowell cut off; more services along the Erewash Valley to serve Ilkeston; and finally of course the Mansfield line with some trains proceeding to Worksop and either continuing to or giving a connection with Retford; this last service might well be restored during the next four years if a portion of new railway is built at Kirkby. Centring on Nottingham all points of the compass were covered.

Prodigious numbers of the 0-4-4 tanks were built at Derby for use on shorter distance local trains, but four coupled tender engines were also employed and the rather ungainly 0-6-4 tanks, nicknamed "Flatirons" put in an appearance. From the 1930s larger engines began to appear in the shape of ex. London Tilbury & Southend Railway tank engines of 4-4-2 wheel arrangement, all three varieties being tried out, and these were quick to identify themselves with Mansfield line workings. The Fowler 2-6-4 tanks ran alongside their younger LMS sisters of similar outline for many years on the Derby–Lincoln trains, but for some reason the Melton route seemed to be their province. The Tilbury tanks shared with, then later gave way to Stanier 2-6-2 tanks to everyone's relief, and these in turn were superseded by the Fairbairn 2-6-4s before Mansfield trains were taken off in October 1964. In the meantime diesel railcars had arrived to monopolize the Lincoln and Derby services, many of the latter now forming through trains to Stoke-on-Trent and Crewe. They also appeared on stopping trains to Leicester and Birmingham. The 1963 summer timetable reveals 11 daily runs to Mansfield one taking the circuitous route via Long Eaton and Pye Bridge, with 6 of the direct trains proceeding to Worksop. The average journey time to Mansfield was 45 minutes which did not compare favourably with the No. 62 bus operated by Trent Motor Traction Co. The Erewash Valley line was served by 18 trains to and 17 from Sheffield, all but one calling at Chesterfield. As against this the Melton line was certainly poorly served with only three stopping trains each way. To Lincoln there were 18 daily trains, 15 of which came through from Derby, but additionally 4 went only as far as Newark, one of these however failing to appear on Saturdays and in school holidays. As might be expected, Derby was abundantly served by 24 runs each day, one of which calls for special mention.

This was the 8pm from Lincoln to Tamworth known for generations as the Tamworth Mail, and indeed it could be traced back to the very earliest

days, its purpose being to effect a northbound connection with the West Coast postal train at the two level Tamworth station, bringing letters and packages from Grimsby and the northerly parts of the old County of Lincoln. In 1963 this train brought a Lincoln based Class B1 each day into Nottingham and in fact the engine continued to Tamworth, returning in the early hours with northbound mail, leaving Nottingham in the opposite direction at 3.43am.

The engine heading the Tamworth Mail displayed one lamp above each buffer thus signifying its classification as an express passenger train and setting it apart from most of the others whose path it followed. It also conveniently introduces the subject of express services which may briefly be examined.

In bygone years the MR, and later the LMS adopted a fairly parochial outlook in the provision of through trains to more distant parts. By that is meant the fact that most such services were to destinations on existing MR routes with relatively few daily trains going through to places which involved the exercise of running powers over the lines of other companies. Therefore, as would be expected, in addition to running trains between Nottingham and London St. Pancras the expresses offered travel to Birmingham, Bristol, Manchester, Sheffield, Leeds and Bradford, all cities where the MR was well established if one accepts that in Manchester it was in partnership with others on the Cheshire Lines Joint Committee. The Scotch expresses have already been referred to of which there were two each to Glasgow and Edinburgh respectively. These trains were run in liaison with Scottish railway companies and prior to 1923 involved the change of locomotive at Carlisle. These four trains comprised two morning departures from St. Pancras and two evening ones offering an overnight service to Scotland. The morning train to Edinburgh, in its final period named "The Waverley" would draw into platform 5 soon after 11.20 and within minutes would be on its way to the Sheffield stop double headed.

The Midland & Great Northern Joint Railway was a quaint organisation with a character all of its own. Its main sphere of operation was in Norfolk and South Lincolnshire but stretching out to Great Yarmouth at one extremity and offering services to Leicester and Nottingham by means of working arrangements with the MR at the other end. The train services between Nottingham and Bourne, South Lynn and other destinations along that line

48 NOTTINGHAM MAR. 10 1904.

10. Nottingham Midland, 10th March 1904. The completed Cab Approach adjacent to the Booking Hall on the Station Street side.

were operated by the Joint Company into Nottingham rather than the other way round, but at least this brought the yellowy brown hybrid locomotive types to add a little variety to the scene. For the most part reaching a destination off the old MR routes therefore involved a change of carriage.

The somewhat unusual combination of the LNWR and M&GN joint railway operating at certain times between Liverpool, Manchester and Yarmouth is covered by means of the illustrations appearing in this book but it would be as well to recall three train services which had specific objectives. The earliest of these in time was the Belfast Boat express which was certainly running in 1911. The train was a late afternoon departure from St. Pancras which called at Nottingham about 7.15pm. In that era prior to the first world war there existed a worthwhile flow of passengers wishing to cross the water to Ireland and the MR made use of its Harbour at Heysham to good purpose offering a nightly service in the comfort of its own trains and vessels. There was a time when the Heysham took an unusual route along the Mansfield branch and beyond to Shirebrook before setting course thence towards Sheffield. The second train worthy of mention was the Summer Saturday's through service to Bournemouth which was particularly a feature of post war years and which ran via the much lamented Somerset and Dorset Joint Railway on whose line it was regularly photographed, frequently headed by the large 2-8-0 engines which Derby built especially for use on that cross country line. This service at Summer Weekends competed with the Newcastle to Bournemouth train which ran daily from Nottingham's other main line station. Finally, there was a drift of population in the 1950's when many of the coal mines in South West Scotland closed and the colliers were offered the opportunity to work in the Nottinghamshire coal field and to move to new houses specially built to accommodate them at the expense of the National Coal Board. In many communities these new houses came to be called "Little Scotland" and for example between Mansfield and Clipstone a large development appeared with street names such as Braemar Road. Many of these colliers raised families in Nottinghamshire but left relatives and friends north of the border. British Railways saw the need for a cheap and reliable service so decided to put on the Friday and Saturday trains between Nottingham and Glasgow which usually ran well filled.

Motive power before the 1930's was much as one would expect. For many years the sturdy and long lived Kirtley 2-4-0 passenger locomotives

were found to be reliable and adequate for the light trains of the day. In the closing years of last century the graceful four coupled designs of Samuel Waite Johnson began to make their presence felt but with train loads increasing the MR chose to go in for double heading rather than produce larger engines, a policy which clearly contributed to the longevity of many engines, often being improved by super heating. To this era belong the graceful single wheelers nicknamed "Spinners" which regularly appeared at the head of the more important trains. Surely no one can deny that the Johnson singles were amongst the most elegant locomotives ever to run in this country and we are indeed fortunate that in the collection of the National Railway Museum that beauty endures still.

Equally famous of course were the Midland Compounds which Mr Johnson introduced towards the end of his term of office and upon which his successor Richard Deeley rested his reputation by improving and multiplying them. Things remained much the same until the end of the independent company period but when the Royal Scot class became established on the West Coast Main Line after 1927 some of the Claughton 4-6-0's were released to take up duties on former Midland Railway Lines which brought large engines into play rather late in the development of locomotive matters as far as Nottingham was concerned. The Claughtons operated from Kentish Town, Nottingham and Leeds taking their turn along with Compounds and other four coupled Midland types on the best expresses, until they in turn gave way to Stanier types in the years preceeding the outbreak of the second world war. The black 5s visited Nottingham and the Jubilee class, known by LMS men as Class 5X came to be allocated to the home shed and forged a connection which lasted until the diesels swept them away. In the final years of steam working rebuilt Royal Scots released from the West Coast line became regular performers with many being allocated to Kentish Town and some, including 46100 *Royal Scot* herself, coming on to the strength of Nottingham Depot.

In the British Railways era some expresses between St. Pancras and Manchester travelled via Nottingham whilst others took the more direct route through Derby. In either case they came to be the preserve of a stud of Britannias freed from duties on other lines and allocated to Trafford Park Shed in Manchester. Regular visitors were 70015 *Apollo*, 70021 *Morning Star* and 70042 *Lord Roberts*. You now have to close your eyes to conjure up these splendid visions from the past.

11. Nottingham Midland, 7th June 1904. Pedestrian entrance to the new station from Station Street. The light penetrating the right hand wall marks the point of one of the entrances from Carrington Street. The protrusion beyond indicates the base of the clock tower.

12. Nottingham Midland, 21st July 1903. At platform level, the middle of the year saw progress with the widening of Carrington Street bridge to accommodate the new station entrance. This was to become platform 5.

13. Nottingham Midland, 7th June 1904. Having been fully operational for some six months, the station is now settling down after its period of disruption, although temporary platform numbers are still in evidence. This view east from platform 6 shows, in particular, the extensive range of goods on offer at the stall of W.H. Smith.

14. Nottingham Midland, 8th August 1904. This view east from platform 3 shows the full effect of the intersection bridge that carried the Great Central Railway's main line over the station. A poster to the right of the platform 4 sign advertises Promenade Concerts, held at the Queens Hall, London, the orchestra being conducted by Mr Henry J. Wood, founder of the famous "Proms" that later transferred to the Albert Hall. *Photo: Author's collection*

15. Nottingham Midland, 8th August 1904. Another view east, with platform 5 to the left, showing the station almost completely finished. This is approximately the same location as that depicted in plate 12, some twelve months earlier. *Photo: Author's collection*

16. Nottingham Midland, 7th June 1904. The new station had been in operation some five months, the facilities for passengers more than adequate at the time this photograph was taken of the Booking Hall. One ticket window at the far end is set aside for First Class business.

17. Nottingham Midland, 17th July 1904. Another view of the Booking Hall but of the opposite side to that seen above.

95 NOTTINGHAM JUNE 7 1904

18. Nottingham Midland, 10th March 1904. Facilities for the travelling public were almost opulent to say the least, as this view of the buffet shows.

49 NOTTINGHAM MAR. 10 1904

19. Nottingham Midland, 10th March 1904. This was the view beneath the large glazed arcade of the cab approach. Entry to the Booking Hall – see plate 16 – was through the first of the smaller arched dooorways.

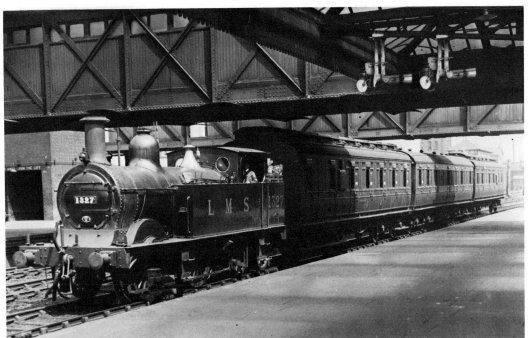

20. Midland, March 1933. The MR breed of 0-4-4T's lived long, many of them lasting into the years of nationalisation. Locally, a couple could be found taking their turns on the Southwell to Rolleston Junction shuttle, they being equipped for push and pull working. The one illustrated, despite looking clean and fit, succumbed in 1940, ending its days working from Derby shed. The 17A shedplate carried by the engine suggests that it is waiting for number 4 platform to become available, and confirms the usefulness of the the middle loops.

Photo: Author's collection

21. Nottingham Midland, c.1927. All the hustle and bustle of the railway at work is present as excursion 747 bound for Blackpool is headed by a Class 4F locomotive getting into its stride and about to blast its exhaust at the underside of Wilford Road Bridge. The tender is stacked high with coal, a situation necessary for such a long journey, and the distant signal is off showing a clear line in the direction of Trent. The larger part of the goods shed , which stands on the site of the first Nottingham Station, is hidden by steam, but it is quite evident that business is brisk judging by the quantity and variety of wagons which fill the sidings. As far as an be ascertained, all the goods rolling stock is of timber construction, including some lettered GW and NE. The low load wagon in the foreground appears to be carrying fairground equipment so we might hazard a guess that the photograph was taken at the end of September just prior to Goose Fair and at a time when trips to Blackpool are at their peak. The substantial but somewhat stark edifice of the Grain Warehouse towers above the goods shed reminding us that Home Ales and Shipstones are long established local brewers.

Photo: courtesy T.G. Hepburn

22. Midland, c.1960. Taken from the footbridge, looking west between the two main island platforms at the time when the track layout included double crossovers between the platform lines and the middle loops, No. 4 platform accommodates a railcar bound for Derby or Leicester as well as a later departure for the Mansfield line. From the operating point of view it made good sense to have two short trains on the same line, and was quite in order when done within station limits, leaving the other face of the island, platform 5, available for an express. However, travellers might have been confused by this practice had it not been for the confident voice of the announcer who made sure, as far as possible, that they boarded the right train.   *Photo: G.H. Platt*

23. Nottingham Midland, c.1959. A high level view looking west showing the goods lines to the left and an express train occupying platform 5. The station clock gives the time as 11.25, suggesting that the train concerned is the *Waverley Express*, a fact confirmed by the coach roofboards, a feature long vanished from the railway scene. The morning service from St. Pancras to Edinburgh came to be known as the Thames–Forth, a name bestowed upon it by the LMS in 1927 but lost for good as a result of the war. This restaurant car express acquired the appropriate title of the *Waverley* in 1957, leaving London at 9.15am and running non-stop at a mile a minute to Nottingham via Melton arriving at 11.18am. Station business now complete it is high time this much lamented train makes further progress along what is now a lost route to the Scottish capital.   *Photo: G.H. Platt*

24. Midland, 20th June 1949. A full head of steam and ready to go, with the six o'clock departure to Worksop, class 3P 4-4-2T No. 41961 of Mansfield shed has a clear road from platform 4. These ex-London, Tilbury & Southend Railway locomotives were not admired by those who had to work them, but despite this, the LMS sent at various times all three varieties of this design to handle the Mansfield trains. Space on the footplate was restricted and the 'penned in' feeling was increased by the low profile of the cab roof. On a hot sticky day with driving wheels too large in diameter to be compatible with the sharp gradients along this subsidence ridden line the working conditions experienced by Mansfield men was in no way pleasant. Nicknamed *Crooners,* they were in fairness unsuited to the area.

Photo: T.J. Edgington

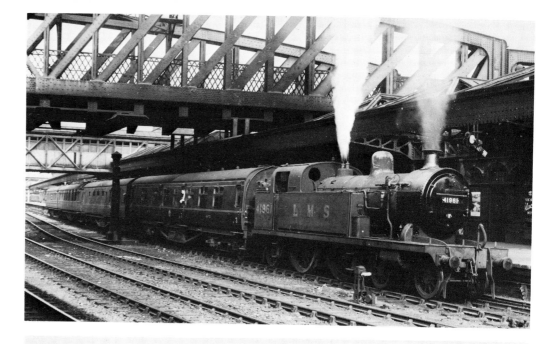

25. Midland, 14th June 1958. Eastern Region motive power to the fore! Class B1 No. 61142 gets the Bournemouth–Cleethorpes train under way, whilst Lincoln's Class A5 No. 69820 will shortly follow the B1 on a stopping train. The Saturdays only express is a further example of a coast to coast working at this station, (The Manchester–Yarmouth already mentioned carried a portion from Liverpool) which traversed the much lamented Somerset & Dorset line, and was probably hauled by one of the splendid 2-8-0 type associated with that line, one of which is based not too far from Nottingham, at the Midland Railway Centre, Butterley.

Photo: J.F. Henton

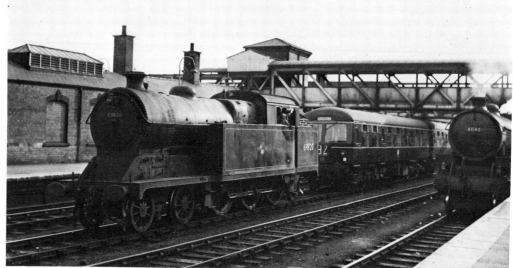

26. Midland, c.1962. A local train from Derby basks in the strong sunlight which catches brand new Sulzer Type 2 (Class 25) diesel completed at Derby Locomotive Works and finished in the attractive two tone green livery.

Photo: D. Dykes

27. Midland, 18th September 1948. Rebuilt Royal Scot, polished and groomed for the occasion, receives new nameplates in the presence of a detachment from the Sherwood Foresters Regiment, whose name it bore, the ceremony taking place on platform 6. *Photo: J.F. Henton*

28. Midland. When looking at this view of the long defunct MIDLAND PULLMAN leaving the carriage sidings after being serviced, it is strange to think that these units had a very limited life, especially when in their basic design they were so clearly the forerunners of the Inter City high speed trains. Initially this train provided Manchester with a quick and comfortable morning service to London St. Pancras, and an evening return at the time when the Manchester to Euston route in course of electrification was subjected to delays. It was quickly realised that the layover in the capital allowed time for a return trip to Nottingham via Leicester. *Photo: J.F. Henton*

29. Midland. Lincoln shed took its turn for many years in working the Derby trains and for this purpose had some interesting classes of locomotive allocated there. The ex. Great Eastern Railway 'Clauds' of Class D16, and GCR tanks engines of Class A5 took their turn as well as the 'Director' class designed by Mr. Robinson of the GCR, at one time the cream of that line's express engines. No. 62666 *Zeebrugge* puts on a display at the head of a Lincoln train passing London Road Junction. *Photo: J.F. Henton*

30. Midland, c.1933. With steam shut off for the last half mile or so downhill into Midland Station, ex M & GN 4-4-0 No. 56 heads a very substantial rake of thirteen coaches, no mean task for a modest four coupled engine over the difficult gradients further east. The length of the train suggests that it may be the Yarmouth–Manchester express, carrying a portion for Liverpool.   *Photo: T.G. Hepburn/Author's collection*

31. Nottingham Midland, c.1933. One of the most photogenic of all LMS express passenger locomotives was the "Baby Scot" class, as it was dubbed, surely evident in this delightful portrait of No. 5916 *E. Tootal Broadhurst* in the infancy of its life standing ready to depart with a St. Pancras express via Melton Mowbray. Sadly this handsome series of engines has failed to secure the attention of preservationists, and indeed, everything in this picture is but a memory, everything that is except that name "Boots". Boots the Chemists remains as a thriving high street business known nationally, having been founded in the Victorian age by one of Nottingham's most eminent benefactors, Jesse Boot, who established the Boots Pure Drug Company, and then found a retail outlet for its products in the chemists stores. He expanded the businesses to such a degree that there was a "Boots" in most midland towns. Gone now are the beautiful mahogany serving counters with rounded ends which were the hallmark of their shops, but it may not be realised that the Company had its own shopfitting department, where, amongst others, carpentry joiners were employed, men who had served a long apprenticeship, and who earned the title of craftsmen. One such man was Bertie Pugh whose home was at Kirkby in Ashfield, and who chose to travel to and from his work by train, which in 1924 was still the most convenient. Illustrated here is a monthly season ticket No. 801, issued to him by the LMS for June 1924, the 3rd class fare being then £1.3.0d. (£1.15). The ticket is pale green and is signed on the reverse by the issuing clerk at Kirkby in Ashfield Station.   *Photo: courtesy T.G. Hepburn*

32. London Road Junction, c.1904. London Road is carried over the railway tracks in this picture looking west, the splendid gantry of signals protecting the eastern approach to the Midland Station. Some 30 signal arms are in view of which 16 no less are carried by the gantry which dominates the scene. The front of the signal arms were painted red and normally carried a white spot as on the distant signal adjacent to the goods lines on the left, which at the period when the photograph was taken was also red, distinguished from others only by the fish tail shape. However, when sited near to main stations the arms carried numbers indicating the track to which they related, as on this occasion, where the upper row of standard size semaphores should be read as relating to two running lines, the first three from the left controlling the southernmost line allowing access to platforms 5 and 6, together with the middle loop running between the two, whilst the remaining five arms relate the next track which was regarded as the main line and giving access to the same three running lines, and additionally platform 4 and the main arms are complemented by the smaller one, beneath, known as hammerhead signals for obvious reasons, and which were used separately for calling on purposes, as for example when the station pilot had to attach a carriage to a train already standing in the departure platform. An oddity of the signalling arrangement was that the upper arm could not be lowered to the clear position unless the corresponding hammerhead signal had first been pulled off. Along the right side of the gantry are 12 more signals of different outline appurtenant to the running lines on the right, these being the main and relief departure lines for the Lincoln and Melton routes. However, it was often necessary to carry out shunting movements close to the station or for an engine to back onto its train which might perhaps be in platform 3 adjacent to Nottingham East Signal Box, visible beyond the road overbridge, and these signals dealt with such movements. The first 9 controlled the main running line which appears to be directly in front of the signal box, and according to the somewhat faded numbers on the individual signals, which can be made out on the original photograph, access could be had from this line to all other lines in the station but platform 6. The northernmost track on the right was controlled by the three remaining signals which permitted reversal only into the sidings, and platforms 1 and 2, the latter being a bay to the right of Nottingham East Box. On the far right, note the unusual position of the balance weight some two thirds of the way up the signal post. Looking through the arches of London Road bridge from left to right, the structure housing the ground frame at the point where the private siding later used by Nixon & Knowles, Timber Merchants, can be seen, whilst under the second arch a goods locomotive takes on water. To the right of this another engine faces the camera as it reposes in platform 4, whilst under the last arch further examples of MR type signals appear to either side of the signal box, these being in pairs denoting that the points could be set for going east or south via Edwalton. Note finally that between the gantry and London Road, the permanent way is carried over the canal.

33. Midland, c.1961. The view eastwards looking from London Road and showing the Low Level Station with its two adjacent tracks, separated by the row of telegraph poles from the ex MR lines, which in turn are bisected by London Road Junction Signal Box. The lines in the centre lead to the Lincoln route and the carriage sidings, whilst the Melton line curves away to the right on its climb towards the River Trent.

Photo: G.H. Platt

34. London Road Junction, c.1959. A recent shower gives a glossy appearance to well creosoted sleepers, and the exhaust from a tank engine running into platform 6 hangs heavy in the air. This elevated view taken from London Road bridge shows to advantage the layout of tracks at the east end of Midland Station. The goods lines on the left were always independently controlled from a signalling point of view, there being through running from London Road Junction and Wilford Road box some distance beyond the station. Nottingham Station East box is of decidedly neglected appearance. Many of the Bradford–St. Pancras expresses paused in platform 3 and water was taken from the crane adjacent to the signal box, thus its elevated frame was needed by the signalman to preserve a reasonable view of the other lines which he was responsible for at such times. By 1959, diesel railcars were much in evidence on the Derby, Lincoln and Leicester stopping trains, one having positioned itself in platform 4 under the bridge which carries the public footpath across the entire layout from Station Street to Queens Road.

35. Midland, c.1953. A stirring sight is provided by Jubilee No. 45560 *Prince Edward Island* getting into its stride with the 8.15am express to London St. Pancras. With a gleaming engine throwing out a generous amount of smoke and steam at the foot of the climb you need only to close your eyes and imagine the sound and the smell of live steam to relive those long lost happy days when this spectacle was routine and hardly remarkable. *Photo: J.F. Henton*

36. Mansfield Junction, c.1913. To borrow a phrase relating to another location, if this were a postcard one could write on the back "just a few lines from Nottingham". This apparently official view was taken from Mansfield Junction signal box to show the contemporary layout looking west with the four tracks of the Derby line going ahead and the route to Mansfield veering off to the right. The single line to the left of the lamp standard gives access to the engine sheds, whilst the land to the left of the telegraph poles has not yet formed the site of the Royal Ordnance Factory. On the right is the commencement of the sidings known as Spike Island.

Photo: Author's collection

37. Lenton April, c.1956. Pride of the Midland Lines for many years were the Midland Compounds or Crimson Ramblers as they were dubbed. The type was introduced in pre-grouping days by the Midland Railway but after 1923 was perpetuated by the LMS in the years before the transformation brought about by Stanier. Nevertheless Compounds penetrated many parts of the LMS system from Bristol to Aberdeen yet remained best loved by men on their parent line who had been weaned on them. Stanier types were in charge of the longer distance expresses by the mid 1950s, supplemented by the BR standard class 5s which were built not so very far away in Derby, thus relegating Compounds to pilot work of which they did a great deal, and some of the shorter distance stopping passenger trains. Although the head code on compound No. 40931 denotes the latter variety the loading of 10 vehicles is to be noted and provides a very respectable loading on the 4.50p.m. departure from Nottingham calling at stations to Bakewell. This train effectively provided an additional service to Derby with plenty of room for those using it but on setting down there, the likelihood is that this train would fill up considerably taking shoppers and workers home along the picturesque Derwent Valley route through the Matlock Bath Gorge and out to Bakewell.

The train is getting in to its stride at Lenton South Junction, southerly point of a triangular connection with the Mansfield Line. The goods lines are unoccupied in this case whilst the line to the right of the view gives access to Nottingham engine sheds. In the background Nottingham Castle stands on a rocky promontory and below that in the picture are the sidings of Nottingham's goods yard known locally as Spike Island.

Photo: T.G. Hepburn

38. Lenton, c.1913. Lines from Mansfield Junction on the right and Lenton South Junction on the left converge by the signal gantry and lead off into the distance towards the site of Lenton Station, the first of those in the area covered by this book to close. The signal arm which is lowered is to permit a train from the Bulwell direction to enter the loop seen on the other contemporary photograph of Mansfield Junction and thereby avoid coming into direct contact with the running lines between Trent and Nottingham. By the 1930s some of the Midland Lines close to the city centre were causing problems for road traffic, which in many cases crossed the railway on the level. Along the Mansfield Line at Bobbers Mill a road bridge was provided in the 1930s and the same remedy was used at this location, the building of the Lenton Abbey road bridge carrying the busy road out to Beeston above the railway tracks at this location. Note the method used here to protect the end of the siding.

Photo: Author's collection

39. Radford, c.1958. Nottingham Shed Class 8F No. 48675 drifts slowly through the station with a Kirkby Sidings to Wellingborough coal train which includes an assortment of wooden bodied wagons commonplace at the time. This train is routed via the Melton line, but much of the tonnage from Kirkby Yards went along the Erewash Valley, first as far as Toton Sidings where it was remarshalled, then by way of Leicester to Glendon Junction near Kettering, where the two routes merged and from which place separate goods lines ran remaining seventy miles or so to Cricklewood in north London. The cleanness of the locomotive compliments the station which has obviously benefitted from a recent repainting in the London Midland Region colours of maroon and cream. The cast iron supports for the up platform awning will be noted as will the absence of unsightly gaps in the decorative timbers. With the closure of Lenton before the First World War, Radford became the first stop for Worksop trains. In this view looking north the junction points are set for the line to Mansfield whilst the line going off left is the eastern end of the short link to the Erewash Valley main line which it joins at Trowell. *Photo: C.A. Hill*

40. Radford, c.1948. Here is the classic Midland line double headed express train of the period with the 3 cylinder "Jubilee" class train engine assisted by a Class 2P 4-4-0, the latter still sporting the initials of its previous owner which ceased to exist at the end of 1947. The train is down Express from St. Pancras to Edinburgh which used the famous Settle to Carlisle line and which afforded Nottingham a direct daily service to the Scottish capital. The name "Waverley" was not given to the train until 1957, but the daytime through train from St. Pancras to Edinburgh had been restored in October 1945 giving a service which approximated to the pre-War "Thames–Forth Express". Simultaneously with the naming of the train came a notable acceleration. By running non-stop to Nottingham at a schedule of a mile a minute the train was due into platform 5 at 11.18am, and further north another non-stop section between Leeds and Carlisle marked a further substantial improvement in overall journey time. Passengers for Glasgow secured a much better connection at Carlisle, and the final section over the border country line which gave the train its name assured an arrival in Edinburgh before 7pm. The formation included a restaurant car, a godsend for those travelling all the way. This photograph shows the 11 coach train on the Radford–Trowell section in a deceptively rural setting. In fact the line, which was in recent years the target for vandals, has remained open despite a mishap at the Trowell end when a merry-go-round coal train ran out of control. *Photo: J.F. Henton*

41. Radford, c.1962. Trip working No. 5 from Nottingham Shed was based at Beeston Sidings on the Derby line, adjacent to the freightliner terminal and, apart from shunting duties in the yards, there would be several forays up the Mansfield branch with empty wagons to keep the collieries supplied. Usually these trips would be to Bestwood Sidings just beyond Bulwell, but sometimes wagons were taken direct to Cinderhill Colliery. Here, LMS built "Jinty" No. 47631 of Nottingham, jogs merrily along north of Radford with a string of steel mineral wagons. A small number of the 350 h.p. diesel shunters were held for use in the main goods yards, but Nottingham Shed always kept a few Jinties on its books, and this one has been fitted with additional rails to the bunker, so adding to its coal capacity for these longer journeys. Strong little machines, they reigned supreme over the diesels on these duties until steam was finally banished. *Photo: C.A. Hill*

42. Basford Vernon, 1st October 1959. In this view of Basford Vernon, Nottingham based 2-6-4T No. 42140 draws in with the 3.07pm Nottingham to Worksop local, whilst in the distance can be seen the depressing but necessary group of buildings which comprise Basford Gas Works. The station, too, is gas lit whilst both platforms are enclosed by the traditional and well known style of diagonal timber fencing typical of the MR and LMS. Entrance to the goods yard is opposite the signal box and leads to about half a dozen sidings, the nearest running to the brick goods shed to the rear to the down platform. Four and a quarter miles from Nottingham, the station enjoyed a weekday service of eleven northbound trains but only nine southbound. Saturday saw an increase in traffic with fourteen trains northbound, one with through carriages to Blackpool on a summer Saturday.
Photo: R.W. Sheppard

43. Basford Vernon, c.1960. A short distance to the north of Basford Vernon lies Lincoln Street level crossing. The road running parallel to the railway line to the right of the picture is the continuation of Vernon Road leading eventually to Bulwell, although Lincoln Street, which crosses the line on the flat, forms part of a through road from Arnold to Stapleford, passing through a busy conurbation on the way. When this photograph was taken the gates would have been opened and closed several times an hour to allow the passing of Mansfield line passenger trains, and an endless procession of coal trains, of fifty wagons at a time, usually headed by a Class 8F from Bestwood, Hucknall and other pits or perhaps from Kirkby yards. That this played havoc with road traffic is an understatement, but today the position has improved by the use of special road signals activated by the signalman. Where the road and railway
continued on next page

43. continued

run together a stone wall about twelve feet high has been built, part of which can be seen beyond the signal box. The chimneys of Watnall brickworks can just be made out on the skyline to the left of the telegraph pole on the west side of the track, but nearer the camera the line passes under the lattice girder bridge of the GNR Derby line. In the top left corner can be seen that company's nine arch brick viaduct.

Photo: Author's collection

44. Basford Vernon, August 1964. The former MR goods yard at Basford Vernon shown signs of neglect to judge by the weed-ridden tracks, although the main line seems to have secured better attention. By the time this photograph was taken time was fast running out for the Mansfield line passenger service and the goods facilities would soon be withdrawn. The factory chimneys in this industrial area on the opposite side of Vernon Road overshadow the station, whilst in the yard Class 4F No. 43951 from Nottingham shed simmers away gently with apparently nothing to do. A couple of open vans have probably brought in some consignments for distribution within the district using the once familiar Scammell lorries, one of which with its trailer can be seen in the distance. These three wheeled vehicles needed to be versatile, taking deliveries to all parts of the city, especially the narrow streets in and around the Lace Market, and it is said of them that they could turn on a sixpence.

Photo: D.H. Beecroft

45. Bulwell Market, 20th June 1961. The parish church of Bulwell presides over the station area as one of Mansfield's sheds long serving tank engines No. 40073 sets off for Nottingham towards the end of its journey which has commenced at Worksop. The station here is on a curve which continues a little way past the Highbury Road overbridge at the far end of the platforms. On this account the signal post visible above the last coach at one time carried arms regulating travel in both directions. Although the station was well located close to the centre of town the goods yard on this occasion derives no benefit whatever from that fact.

Photo: J. Cupit

46. Bulwell Market, 30th March 1959 This photograph is taken from the main road overbridge at the north end of the station where the morning train from Nottingham to Worksop is calling for a few moments as required by the timetable. It was only possible to obtain a reasonable photograph from this position during the course of the morning for even here the scene is back-lit as the shadows cast across the up platform prove. Nevertheless the light does afford the opportunity to see much of the architectural detail, at this location exactly 129 miles from St. Pancras. The increasing use of diesel railcars elsewhere freed the more powerful 2-6-4Ts to work this line during the final years until the passenger trains were withdrawn in October 1964 rendering Mansfield the largest town in England in terms of population without a rail service. There is now a strong proposal to reintroduce an hourly service between Nottingham and Retford via Mansfield and Worksop but if this is to materialise then firstly the finance must be forthcoming, and secondly a new section of line is required at Kirkby-in-Ashfield. If things promised come to pass Bulwell Market may rise like a phoenix from the ashes to be given a new opportunity to prove that travel by rail is the in thing and certainly better than trying to find a car parking space in the city.

Photo: J. Cupit

47. Bulwell, 31st August 1963. On Summer Saturdays the holiday trains were an important and interesting feature in the passenger timetables, not least because during the course of a journey to the coast the regional boundary would be crossed, which often gave the chance of seeing a locomotive unusual to a particular location. Furthermore, several junctions existed between the various pre-grouping railway systems and quite often the itinerary involved passing through at least one such junction. Egginton to the west of Derby, Shirebrook to the north of Mansfield, Lincoln St. Mark's and Sneinton Junction in Nottingham all spring to mind. For example it could be difficult to get from the LMS Lines in the Nottingham area to Skegness or Mablethorpe unless the cumbersome manoeuvre at Sneinton was undergone. On the other hand if the destination were Cleethorpes a straight run through Lincoln St. Mark's presented no problem. The train depicted here is the 8.32am Nottingham Midland to Scarborough train, planned to run via Mansfield no doubt to enable passengers living in the Bulwell and Hucknall areas to join the train near their homes. Standard Class 5 No. 73140 gets a helping hand from a tank engine more usually employed on the local passenger services. No. 42587 will assist as far as Kirkby-in-Ashfield from which point gradients favour the train. At Shirebrook the eastern curve to Warsop Junction will be used followed by the north curve at Tuxford where the East Coast Main Line will be reached. The train engine is passing beneath the Great Central's Bulwell viaduct which seems to be occupied by fish empties for Hull or Grimsby, which means that the paths taken by the two trains in view will be bound to cross each other once more.

Photo: T.G. Hepburn

Table **214**—

NOTTINGHAM AND WORKSOP

WEEKDAYS ONLY

Miles							SO		SO	SO		SX		SO		SX				SX	SO
		a.m.	a.m.	a.m.	a.m.	a.m.	a.m.	a.m.	p.m.	p.m.	p.m.	p.m.		p.m.	p.m.	p.m.		p.m.		p.m.	p.m.
0	**NOTTINGHAM Midland** dep.	.	5 47	7 25	8 40	9 45	...	11 46	12 25	...	3 11	4 40	...	4 40	5 11	5 14		6 7	...	9 25	10 15
2¼	Radford	...	5 52	7 30	...	9 50	.	.	12 30	.	3 16	4 45	.	4 45	5 17	.		6 12	.	.	.
5¼	Bulwell Market	.	6 2	7 39	8 49	9 57	...	...	12 37	...	3 24	4 52	...	4 52	5 25	...		6 19	...	...	...
8¼	Hucknall Byron	...	6 13	7 47	8 57	10 5	.	12 0	12 45	.	3 32	5 0	.	5 0	5 33	.		6 27	.	9 40	10 30
9¼	Linby	.	...	7 51	9 0	...	...	...	...	...	3 35	5 4	...	5 4	5 36	...		6 30	...	9 44	10 34
10¾	Newstead	...	6 20	7 57	9 4	10 11	.	12 6	12 51	.	3 39	5 10	.	5 10	5 40	.		6 34	.	9 50	10 40
13¼	Kirkby-in-Ashfield East	.	6 29	8 6	9 12	10 19	...	12 14	12 59	...	3 47	5 19	...	5 19	5 48	6 20	via Pye Bridge	6 42	...	9 59	10 49
14¾	Sutton Junction	...	6 33	8 10	9 16	10 23	.	12 18	1 3	.	3 51	5 23	.	5 23	5 52	6 24		6 46	.	10 3	10 53
17¼	Mansfield Town arr.	.	6 38	8 15	9 21	10 28	...	12 23	1 8	...	3 56	5 28	...	5 28	5 57	6 29		6 51	...	10 8	10 58
	Mansfield Town dep.	5 30	6 48	.	.	10 34	11 30	12 28	.	2 22	4 1	5 34	.	.	6 5	.		6 56	.	.	11 4
18¾	Mansfield Woodhouse	5 34	6 52	...	...	10 38	11 34	12 32	...	2 26	4 5	5 38	...	...	6 9	...		7 0	...	...	11 8
21¾	Shirebrook West	5 44	6 59	.	.	10 45	11 41	12 39	.	2 33	4 12	5 45	.	.	6 16	.		7 7	.	.	11 15
23	Langwith	5 49	7 4	...	...	10 49	11 45	12 43	...	2 37	4 16	5 50	...	...	6 20	...		7 11	...	...	11 20
25½	Elmton & Creswell	5 55	7 10	.	.	10 55	11 51	12 49	.	2 43	4 22	5 56	.	.	6 26	.		7 17	.	.	11 26
27¾	Whitwell	6 0	7 15	...	...	10 59	11 55	12 53	...	2 48	4 26	6 0	...	...	6 30	...		7 21	...	...	...
32	**WORKSOP** arr.	6 11	7 26	.	.	11 10	.	1 4	.	2 59	4 42	...	.	.	6 44	.		7 32	.	.	.

Miles			XS											SO	SX	SO					
		a.m.	a.m.	a.m.		a.m.	a.m.		a.m.	a.m.		a.m.		p.m.	p.m.	p.m.		p.m.	p.m.	p.m.	p.m.
0	**WORKSOP** dep.	...	...	...		...	6 30	...	...	8 15	...	11 25	...	...	...	1 30	...	3 47	5 32	7 7	8 7
4¼	Whitwell	.	.	.		.	6 42	.	.	8 27	.	11 37	.	12 32	.	1 42	.	3 59	5 45	7 19	8 19
6½	Elmton & Creswell	...	...	...		...	6 47	...	7 32	8 32	...	11 42	...	12 37	...	1 47	...	4 4	5 50	7 24	8 24
9	Langwith	.	.	.		.	6 52	.	7 37	8 37	.	11 47	.	12 42	.	1 52	.	4 9	5 55	7 29	8 29
10¼	Shirebrook West	...	...	...	via Pye Bridge	...	6 56	...	7 41	8 42	...	11 51	...	12 46	...	1 56	...	4 13	5 59	7 33	8 33
13¼	Mansfield Woodhouse	.	.	.		.	7 2	.	7 46	8 48	.	11 57	.	12 51	.	2 2	.	4 19	6 5	7 39	8 39
14¾	Mansfield Town arr.	...	...	...		...	7 8	...	7 52	8 54	...	12 3	...	12 57	...	2 8	...	4 25	6 11	7 45	8 45
	Mansfield Town dep.	5 40	.	5 59		6 40	7 11	.	7 55	8 58	.	12 8	.	1 2	1 2	.	.	4 30	6 19	.	8 51
17¼	Sutton Junction	5 46	...	6 5		6 45	7 17	...	8 0	9 4	...	12 14	...	1 7	1 7	...	...	4 36	6 25	...	8 57
18¾	Kirkby-in-Ashfield East	5 51	.	6 10		6 49	7 22	.	8 4	9 9	.	12 19	.	1 11	1 11	.	.	4 41	6 30	.	9 2
21¼	Newstead	5 57	...	.		6 55	7 28	...	8 10	9 15	...	12 25	...	1 17	1 17	...	...	4 47	6 36	...	9 8
22¾	Linby	6 1	.	...		6 58	7 32	.	8 13	.	.	.	.	1 20	1 20	.	.	4 51	.	.	.
23¾	Hucknall Byron	6 4	...	.		7 1	7 35	...	8 16	9 20	...	12 30	...	1 23	1.23	...	...	4 54	6 41	...	9 13
26¾	Bulwell Market	...	.	...		7 7	7 41	.	8 22	9 26	.	12 36	.	1 29	1 29	.	.	5 1	6 47	.	9 19
29¾	Radford	6 14	...	.		7 14	7 48	.	8 29	9 33	.	.	.	1 36	1 36	.	.	5 8	6 54	.	.
32	**NOTTINGHAM Midland** arr.	6 20	.	7 16		7 20	7 56	...	8 35	9 39	...	12 46	...	1 42	1 42	...	...	5 15	7 0	...	9 29

SO—Saturdays only.
SX—Saturdays excepted.
TC—Through Carriages.

48. Edwalton, c.1936. Heavy civil engineering works are apparent judging the depth of the cutting and the size of the concrete drainage channel near to Edwalton. Two locomotives are deemed necessary to head this nine coach train probably bound for Yarmouth. The train engine is Fowler 2-6-2T No. 2338 but the leading engine is burning up coal from its home shed of South Lynn, the smoke display coming from M&GN Joint Railway locomotive No. 53 which, despite having all the characteristics of a Midland engine, eventually fell into LNER Class D54 when that company absorbed the M&GN on 1 October 1936. By virtue of its status as a joint line, the M&GN was well placed to offer Leicester as well as Nottingham a daily through service to east Anglia and specifically to Great Yarmouth. Nottingham had four trains per day to the M&GN line, the afternoon express generally departing around 3.10.   *Photo: T.G. Hepburn*

49. Edwalton, 6th June 1953. Edwalton Station is in the right background as the morning businessmans train from Nottingham to St. Pancras hurries through under clear signals. Nottingham shed's Class 5XP Jubilee No. 45560 *Prince Edward Island* in immaculate external condition, heads a rake of spotlessly clean coaches on the service which in later years was called "The Robin Hood", so identifying it as the premier express of the day. In 1960 "The Robin Hood" is shown in the public timetable as leaving Nottingham at 8.15am Monday to Friday and due into St. Pancras at half past ten.

Photo: T.G. Hepburn

50. Edwalton, 2nd May 1959. Taking the long 1 in 200 climb in fine style as it enters Edwalton Cutting is Royal Scot Class No. 46158 *The Loyal Regiment* on the 8.15 Nottingham to St. Pancras on a bright Saturday morning. The strong south westerly wind forces the exhaust downwards but the engine is well in command of the situation as the safety valves lift. This picture conveys the impression of supreme confidence for the task ahead, and so it was for the football team whose supporters it was carrying for on this day Nottingham Forest F.C. carried off the F.A. Cup beating Luton Town at Wembley.

Photo: J.F. Henton

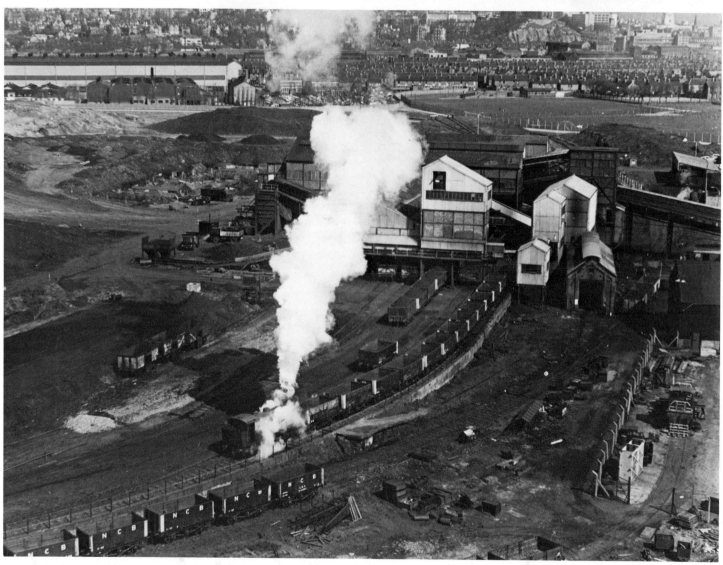

51. Clifton Colliery, 8th April 1968. The last regular steam locomotive working in the city of Nottingham was at Clifton Colliery. The National Coal Board, appropriately enough when one thinks about it, continued to use steam traction longer than British Railways in the area and although industrial steam at National Coal Board locations went on for several years afterwards, many of the locomotives so used were six coupled saddle tanks of the same general specification. One such, *Philip*, shunts empty wagons under the screens in this unusual view taken from the roof of Wilford Power Station. By chance some of the more familiar landmarks of the city of Nottingham are captured on the sky line, the castle and council house being instantly recognisable.

Photo: M.S. Castledine

52. Nottingham Shed, 28th April 1957. The breakdown train finds itself parked as usual on one of the shed roads to the west of the main buildings. The steam crane is a product of Cowan's and Sheldon of Carlisle and was strategically placed to attend to any mishap on the several lines radiating from Nottingham. A glance at the map reveals the existence of many important junctions and it takes only a little imagination to picture the chaos, should certain of them be fouled. One amusing mishap, though the driver of the engine concerned did not see it that way, cleared up by Nottingham's break-down gang was the occasion when an 8F nose-dived into the turntable pit at Kirkby-in-Ashfield shed. Double-heading of coal trains leaving Kirkby Sidings was commonplace so quite often 2 engines required for such a working would visit the shed's turntable together. The 8F had been turned and then parked in a head shunt beyond the table whilst the 4F which was to act as pilot took its turn. Unfortunately when the latter was half turned the 8F started to roll forward because the brake had not been applied. The result was obvious. This incident has been immortalised by Bret Stevens, once employed at Kirkby sheds, in one of his delightful ballads from which the following quote is taken: "They fetched the gang from Nottingham and soon they set about, with chains and jacks and dirty words they got the damn thing out".

Returning to the illustration the overhead coaler peeps out above the make-shift vehicles of the breakdown train whilst its much older counterpart appears somewhat neglected beyond the approach ramp. The entrance to one of Nottingham's four linked round houses beckons in the distance, a strange name this, for most round houses were actually square. The depot could in no way be described as cramped but, as with most engine sheds, it was impossible to accommodate the entire allocation undercover, more so at weekends, when many goods workings did not run. The lines of engines stood outside were therefore inevitable.

The depot covered the whole range of train workings from express passenger through humdrum stopping trains and from fast fitted goods trains through the whole spectrum down to the humble shunter, and as such its allocation was large. It is perhaps surprising to find that in 1950, purely in terms of numbers, its allocation was only surpassed amongst London Midland Region Sheds by Newton Heath, Toton and Saltley. Towards the end of that year if one excludes diesel shunters of which Nottingham had a

few, its allocation of 139 engines included 6 compounds, a type long associated with the shed, including No. 40929; a dozen class 2P tender engines handled the middle distance stopping turns including some workings on the Mansfield line and also involved themselves in pilot work. Three small Stanier Nos. 40120/40/78 ventured occasionally onto the Mansfield line but 6 of the earlier Tilbury tanks were also earning their crust in the same manner. Eleven larger tank engines with the 2-6-4 wheel arrangement had the extra coal and water capacity required for workings to Lincoln, Derby, Leicester and down the Melton Line. Half a dozen Black 5s came in handy for working the less arduous London trains on which the star performers were the 5 'Jubilees', 2 of which were called respectively *Uganda* and *Hong Kong*, these remaining on the books for a good many years. Most of the shunting was entrusted to the diesels and the Jinties but these were ably assisted by 5 ancient 2Fs, Nos. 58133/5 and 58201/48/52. There were however 3 strangers in the camp in the shape of ex-Lancashire & Yorkshire Railway goods engines, 52121/3/35, one of which could usually be found pottering around into the sidings within sight and sound of the engine shed. Most of the goods workings were covered by the familiar 3Fs, 4Fs and 8Fs, generous numbers of each operating from Nottingham, but the 3Fs also took a hand in passenger workings when required, once more the Mansfield line attracting them, and the 4Fs would range further afield when they put in some time on excursion work. The complement of steam engines was made up by 3 Johnson tanks, Nos. 41682/6 and 41846, one of these normally being the shed pilot, and the 2 passenger tanks Nos. 58050/6 retained for the Southwell to Rolleston Junction push and pull service.

Five years earlier Nottingham had been the home to a famous engine, now preserved. LMS No. 2 was the last survivor of the famous Kirtley double-framed passenger engines with 6'3" driving wheels and on withdrawal it was reserved for preservation and was initially restored in 1948 as No. 158A in the old MR numbering. As such the locomotive still survives and affords a visible reminder of a Victorian locomotive with strong local connections. By January 1963 the number of steam engines based at Nottingham had declined to no more than 80, predominantly 4Fs and 8Fs, but with a few passenger tanks and Black 5s supplemented by 10 Crabs. By this date the 2Ps, the Compounds and even the Jubilees found no home here.

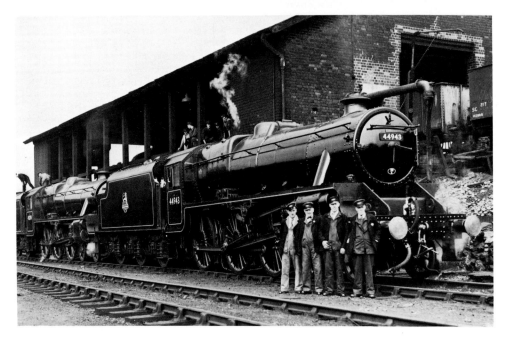

53. Nottingham MPD, 5th July 1955. It would appear that Nottingham was blessed with fair weather on the occasion of this royal visit to the city. Certainly the two Stanier Class 5 locomotives are gleaming in their BR lined black livery as they slow down for the station and pass Mansfield Junction, the signals indicating a clear road ahead.

The main purpose of the visit by Her Majesty the Queen and the Duke of Edinburgh was to attend the Royal Show, the yearly agricultural gathering which used to be staged at various venues around the country, and in 1955 was put on in the grounds of Wollaton Hall.

The train had been stabled overnight on the North Curve at Trent, and therefore approached the station from the west. The signals above the second locomotive control Mansfield line train. Observe the four headlamps carried by the leading engine, which is the special code reserved for use when royalty is aboard the train. *Photo: T.G. Hepburn*

54. Nottingham MPD, 5th July 1955. This photograph may be out of sequence, for it is difficult to say if the engines are arriving or leaving the shed. Evidence for the latter theory is the signal on the left being in the off position and the headlamps on the bufferbeam being correctly placed for the pair to proceed towards Midland Station once out onto the main line. It matters not really, for in any event, the picture illustrates two highly polished locomotives, a joy to behold, and not an everyday sight in 1955 when staff shortages at many BR depots resulted in fewer hands available to keep the paintwork clean. As well as controlling the junction with the Mansfield line the signal box stood at the entrance to the engine shed, thus guarding the main Nottingham to Derby line as well. *Photo: T.G. Hepburn*

55. Nottingham MPD, 5th July 1955. Whilst the city was honoured by the royal visitor the two Class 5 locomotives 44943 and 45274 were detached from the train and came on Nottingham shed to use the facilities there. The brick coaling stage with its pitched roof stands high above the engines as they take on coal and water in preparation for the return journey. Two railwaymen pay careful attention to the stacking of coal on 45274 whilst the footplate crews pose for the camera in front of the highly polished leading engine. *Photo: T.G. Hepburn*

56. Nottingham MPD, 5th July 1955. A closer look at Black 5 No. 44943. Whilst locomotives of this type were allocated to Nottingham Shed and could therefore be seen regularly, it was not every day that one clean as a new pin would turn up and command the admiration of the workers in the coaling stage. The engine clearly has a good head of steam, and royal train headlamp code has been restored to mark the occasion as the depots top brass pose for a souvenir photograph to record the event. The gentleman on the left is Mr. Thompson, the shedmaster wearing his trilby as always, and standing alongside him is believed to be the Inspector who travelled with the train. This series of photographs was made possible due in large extent to one of the authors, who lived near and was on friendly terms with Mr. Thompson. Hearing almost at the last minute that the royal train was to visit Nottingham, for such services have always been operated under conditions of security with notices being sent out to the general railway staff only shortly before the run, the author's suggestion that the train should be photographed by Gordon Hepburn, perhaps the best known of the local railway cameramen, found favour, the price paid doubtless being copies all round. *Photo: T.G. Hepburn*

57. Lenton, 5th July 1955. While the two royal train engines were taking on coal and water, the eleven coach train, for some reason which is not clear, was turned. This is all the more strange when it is realised that on departure the train did not retrace its route, but rather took the Melton Mowbray line and returned to St. Pancras via Manton. However, Class 8F No. 48709 of Nottingham shed shows signs of being not long out of works as it enjoys a break from more mundane duties and finds itself at the head of the royal train stock passing the engine sheds on the main line, proudly bearing express headlamp code, which is correct for royal train empty coaching stock, and approaching the triangle comprising Mansfield Junction and Lenton North and South Junctions, by which means the objective was achieved. *Photo: Author's collection*

58. Edwalton, 5th July 1955. To compare this photograph with the first one in this group will establish that the train has indeed been turned for the coach attached to the 8F in the last picture is now at the head of the train as it climbs through Edwalton conveying the royal party back to London. The engines may well have been specially selected for the job as being the last two fresh from Crewe Works having completed their running in trails but after this brief interlude in the limelight they might well have returned to ordinary traffic never again to have quite the same attention paid to their appearance. After this day they became just two out of a class of 842 similar locomotives.

Photo: T.G. Hepburn

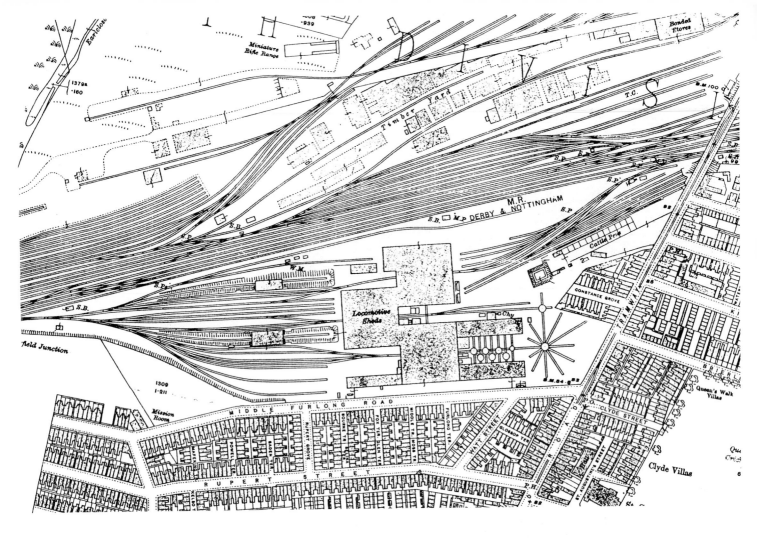

59. Nottingham Shed, July 1938. The sidings at the west end of Nottingham sheds are well filled with wagons containing loco coal whilst in the middle background stands the water tank to provide supplies of that other vital raw material needed to feed a locomotive boiler. The Stanier class 8F even in 1938 would be nothing remarkable but this particular locomotive is note-worthy because it never carried British Railway's number. It appears here as LMS No. 8071, but during the second world war it was taken into military service by the War Department where it was numbered 617. Unfortunately the locomotive was destined to have a short life being lost while on active service. *Photo: W. Potter*

60. Radcliffe-on-Trent, 1949. In the first period of nationalisation several quite new Thompson class L1 tanks appeared on the Grantham services and as time went by more were drafted in which widened their sphere of influence, particularly to the Pinxton branch and to the Sutton-in-Ashfield service when it was resurrected for a short time in 1956. With BRITISH RAILWAYS in full on the tank sides a commendably clean No. 67758 eases into the pleasant station at Radcliffe-on-Trent. One person who is very conscious of the camera and is glad to see the train arrive may be travelling, but is that a pigeon basket he is carrying?
Photo: Author's collection

61. Saxondale Junction, 4th September 1962. East of Radcliffe-on-Trent the track was quadruple as far as Saxondale Junction whose signals enclose this light-weight Derby Friargate to Grantham service scurrying along behind class L1 No. 67780. The configuration of posts and arms is not quite symmetrical as might appear at first glimpse, the more clumsy arrangement to the left necessitating the provision of an additional platform below the signal area. Saxondale is the junction where the line to Melton Mowbray North left the Grantham route. *Photo: Author's collection*

62. Colwick, 1957. The signal gantry heralds the imminent splitting of the lines into three distinct routes. In point of fact Rectory Junction was so close to the river that some shunting operations took the engines actually across the bridge. This has happened with class J52 No. 68829 now pushing its train into a fairly stiff westerly wind. From left to right the three main posts carry signals for Nottingham, Colwick Yards, and Gedling respectively. The view is downstream and time was when the Trent Navigation Authority was careful enough to insist upon a bridge designed to give both width and height to meet maritime requirements, especially taking into account the need for masts to get through when the river was running high. Upstream from this point the National Watersports Centre has been established in recent times. *Photo: F.A. Quayle*

63. Netherfield and Colwick, 26th March 1966. The pedestrian entrance to the Station was by means of the road overbridge at the western end of the platforms which were, unusually for this line, constructed on the island principle. The old station had boasted a long overall canopy roof on both sides of the buildings which went down the centre of the platform but this fell into disrepair in earlier years and the opportunity was taken to modernise the station by providing a singularly unattractive flat roofed structure not very far removed from the Portacabin idea. Concrete lamp standards with horizontal enclosed fluorescent lights announcing the name of the station were necessary here to illuminate the atrocious surface to the platforms, a feature very evident on this rain swept occasion. A very clean Class 8F number 48467 in charge of a special working is the only feature here to relieve the otherwise depressing scene.

64. The Hall, n.d. The tree-lined slopes of Colwick woods protect the north side of the line at The Hall sidings which were located between Trent Lane Junction and Netherfield Station. The line at this point keeps fairly close company with the Lincoln route of the Midland Railway, and to the south of both could be found Colwick Race Course. Even now the Nottingham races are held at Colwick with both daytime and evening meetings, but gone are the days when excursion trains drew into the platform at Race Course Station, disgorging the many punters who hoped for a little win to make the day worth while. The signal box at the Hall supervised the sidings illustrated here as well as the special race meeting trains, whilst on this occasion class J52 No. 68853 rattles by with a transfer trip destined for the nearby yards at Low Level. *Photo: P.J. Lynch*

65. Colwick Yards, 21st April 1951. With the long white pole resting on his shoulder one could well imagine that the shunter spent some time as a young lad in the Brigade of Guards. The pole takes the place of a rifle, the right arm is swinging and there is no sign of anything other than a straight back in the manner of his walking. Indeed he and his colleagues would walk miles up and down the sidings coupling wagons together here, separating them there, noting the places of consignment on the tickets conveniently affixed to the bottom corner of the trucks at eye level and making sure that each wagon got into the correct siding. Wooden bodied wagons of various capacities still rule the roost and the trip engine is vintage GN. Class J5 No. 65487 belongs to a class of 20 engines all surviving nationalisation and most of them being allocated to Colwick during their final years. It was a J5 pottering about in the goods yard at Sutton-in-Ashfield Town adjacent to Priestsic Road Schools, and particularly the turning of the wheels, which first captured the imagination of one of the authors in January 1949 and that attraction to the railway has proved fatal. *Photo: J.F. Henton*

66. London Road Low Level Station, c.1959. The canal in the foreground runs parallel with and adjacent to the thoroughfare known as London Road from which this view is obviously taken. The terminus here was opened on 3/10/1857 and the building survives to the present day having recently been externally restored though not completely refurbished. A local architect, T.C. Hine, designed the station, some say incorporating East Croft Hall, but most people would dispute this and prefer the view that the architecturally attractive part of the building coincides with the coming of the GNR into the city. It is obvious from this photograph that later additions have somewhat spoiled the effect not the least of which is the 2 storey portion with overhanging pitched roof seemingly tagged on as an after-thought. This was the location for Nottingham Control Office until it was based in Victoria Station and is younger than the remainder of the station. One thing that can be said with certainty is that this station is the most beautiful legacy left by that important railway with the long name, the Ambergate, Nottingham & Boston & Eastern Junction Railway. *Photo: G.H. Platt*

67. (below) London Road, Low Level, 1945. During the second world war every one of the home railway companies played its part in contribution to the war effort, sometimes by building tanks and other vehicles for army use, frequently in ferrying about troops and their equipment, and daily by the transporting of ammunition and materials to where they were required. Another daily effort required of the railway, totally unsung, but nevertheless vital in maintaining morale was the handling of the mail on behalf of the Army Post Office. The central depot required to which all mail addressed to members of the armed forces could be sent resulted in London Road Low Level Station being the departure point for the army mail train. The Army Post Office Centre was set up in Nottingham where men and women on the ATS did a tremendous job of re-sorting letters and parcels so they would get to the right unit and indeed to the addressee in person. Although the train did not run every day there were doubtless many weeks when it did so, and fortunately one such occasion has been caught by the camera, where LNER class K3 No. 28 is setting off for a secret destination which would doubtless have been one of the channel ports. About 300 bags of mail, each containing 100 items or so, could be accommodated in a covered wagon, about 20 of which form this particular train formation with a six wheel vehicle bringing up the rear.

One of the busiest times would surely have been from April 1944 onwards when massive numbers of troops soon to be involved in the D-Day landings were moved to secret quarters known to Army Commanders and Army Post Office Staff alone. Mail addressed to these fighting men and women was accumulated in Nottingham to be sent overseas after 6th June and thereafter as territory was gained in France and the low countries the batallions were constantly on the move, keeping the people engaged in sorting the mail right on their toes. It is said that well over 1½ million bags of mail were despatched from here in the four years down to May 1945. In that last year the schedule was for the train to depart after dark at 10.20pm and to join the Southern Railway at Kensington to give an arrival at Dover at 6.30 the following morning. Doubtless over the years the route taken by this train would not have remained constant and it is known for example that at one period it travelled via Melton Mobray North and Northampton. Thus did the LNER in Nottingham in a small but important way contribute towards the eventual victory. *Photo: Author's collection*

68. London Road Low Level, 1934. Afternoon sun lights up the front of George V class express locomotive built to the designs of Bowen-Cooke, standing at the Southern-most platform after arrival from Northampton with a stopping train. The engine is No. 5376 *Snipe*, formerly LNW No. 1730, the photograph being taken before the surviving members of the class received the No. 2 prefix to distinguish them from new LMS construction of Black 5s. Although a terminal station, it boasted 7 platform faces, a facility it never warranted even in its busiest days. The 1939 Bradshaw reveals 5 trains in each direction between Nottingham and Northampton departing from Nottingham respectively at 6.57am., 8.50am, 10.42am, 2.50pm and 6.25pm. Of these the second morning departure collected a coach at Melton Mowbray which ran through to London Euston being attached to an up express at Northampton. This coach returned on the last down train of the day being detached at Melton Mowbray before the remaining vehicles continued to Nottingham. The use of Low Level station for the Northampton service continued until 1944 when it was diverted into Victoria. Right at the end of the pre-grouping era one other passenger train started its journey here, namely the first morning train of the day to Newstead along the Leen Valley line. That train ran via Gedling and Daybrook at which point passengers from Nottingham Victoria and, strangely enough, London Road High Level, having travelled non-stop over the Suburban Railway on a Pinxton train, could change stations to Newstead. This is borne out by entry in the reprint on the July 1922 Bradshaw which shows no corresponding service terminating at London Road Low Level. In the years between the two world wars, if you wanted to see unusual locomotive power and a curious collection of rolling stock then this was the place to come. Mention has been made elsewhere of the forces mail trains from London Road and in later years it has continued to find use as a parcels depot, but a brief look back to its more illustrious years when the station could boast 4 departures in the space of 15 minutes is worth while. During the final months of the nineteenth century, just before the wholesale transfer of GNR train services to the brand new Victoria Station, London Road as it was then known accommodated nearly all the GNR domestic services on that company's lines west of Grantham.

Starting with the 5.30am to Pinxton via Gedling and culminating with the 11.20pm to Skegby via the Nottingham Suburban Line, a total of 58 departures appeared on the timetable if one excludes the trains which only ran on certain days of the week and the four Manchester to Kings Cross expresses calling at Highlevel Station, which at that time was referred to as "Newstation". The second and third trains of the day were respectively the 5.35 to Grantham and the 5.48 to Stafford via Gedling, then the station went back to sleep until the 7 o'clock train set out for Newark. The four departures in 15 minutes referred to started at 7.45am with the workmen's train via Gedling which only went as far as Daybrook. Ten minutes later the Grantham Express departed followed at an interval of only 2 minutes by the first train of the day going through to Burton-on-Trent via the suburban line. At 8 o'clock the London and North Western company's parliamentary train calling at all stations to Northampton commenced its tedious journey. Every one of the Leen Valley trains went via Thorney Wood but it will be noted at this date the line beyond Skegby did not yet boast a passenger service. Trains to Pinxton and to Derby and beyond for the most part went via Gedling but the odd one or two availed themselves of the shorter but steeper route over the Suburban Line. On Wednesdays only there was an 8.55am train to Boston, on Saturdays an early afternoon train ran to Heanor whilst every day of the week there were departures at 2.50pm and 5.45pm to Eggington Junction, neither of the trains bothering to go forward either to Burton-on-Trent or to Stafford, doubtless because reasonable connections could be made with other company's trains at the limit of the service. At this date the London and North Western Company operated six trains to Northampton but only the 9am departure is described as an express. On Sundays all trains going beyond Daybrook used the longer route via Gedling, but from a total of 15 departures none served Newark, Stafford or Northampton and the 2 trains up the Leen Valley penetrated n o further than Sutton-in-Ashfield. Low level Station claims for itself a strange distinction out of the city's three main establishments of being for most of its life the most poorly patronised yet at the same time it is far away the longest surviving.   *Photo: T.G. Hepburn*

69. London Road Low Level, c.1952. Destination perhaps Sutton-on-Sea or Mablethorpe. Excursion No. 964 gets on the move again behind Colwick B1 No. 61131 having negotiated the double reversal where the two routes run parallel adjacent to Meadow Lane. The date is believed to be Good Friday, the Easter period always being regarded as the beginning of the season when a dozen or more "seasiders" ran from stations throughout the East Midlands. Class J6 No. 64215 awaits the next train from Coalville to Skegness. Drivers and firemen based at Colwick were usually quite keen to work these trains for they too had a free day at the coast and this brings to mind one amusing aside. On a particular day at the weekend Colwick men with their engines had worked several trains into Skegness and some had doubtless quenched their thirsts in the towns pubs during the afternoon. Having gone back to the railway station to pick up the return workings one erstwhile driver was observed in some state of intoxication but nevertheless sleeping without a care in the world. He was obviously in no fit state to be on duty so his colleagues decided to bed him down comfortably in the first coach and see that he got home safely. Having stopped the train at Netherfield a workmate escorted the driver to his home in the locality by which time it was about midnight. The door was locked and the lights were out but the persistent banging aroused a neighbour who remarked to the effect that nobody was at home as they had all gone to Skeggy for the week!

70. London Road Low Level, c.1930. Francis William Webb, benefactor to the town of Crewe yet at the same time autocrat in locomotive affairs of the London and North Western Railway designed and built some extraordinary locomotives. Some were poor things held in low regard by the men who drove them but others, usually those of simple robust construction, enjoyed a long life. Of the latter type the 'Precedent' class built between 1874 and 1901 earned many honours in the Anglo Scottish Races at the end of the last century, of which LNW No. 790 *Hardwicke* has been preserved. Of the same type LMS No. 5000 *Princess Beatrice*, by now relegated to duties well away from the main line, holds centre stage in this period piece departing with a Northampton train. The last member of the class was withdrawn from service in 1934 but in the age of preservation we have been treated to the sight of *Hardwicke* restored to shining black and indeed working.

Photo: T.G. Hepburn

71. Sneinton Junction, 14th July 1963. At the end of 1964 the connection between the Lincoln and Grantham lines at Netherfield was restored after an absence of almost 100 years and this very simple piece of engineering work facilitated through running between Nottingham Midland and points west thereof to Grantham, Boston and Skegness. The new connection at Netherfield was first used for passenger traffic from 10th January 1965 from which date, on Sunday's only, the Grantham trains used it. Before the connection was restored the difficult rail layout at Lincoln, which at that time included 2 level crossings in quick succession on the High Street, prevented the use of the route through Lincoln St. Mark's for excursions to the Lincolnshire coast other than those destined for the Cleethorpes area. The train shown here headed by 2-6-4T No. 42184 has originated at Leicester London Road and is making its way to Skegness. The train is about to cross Meadow Lane which remains to this day a level crossing, before setting back through the reverse connection into the yards at London Road Low level, the points being actually concealed by the locomotive. Once the coaches have been drawn back the Eastern Region engine already waiting patiently will attach itself for the remainder of the journey, whilst the ex-LMS locomotive will presumably adjourn to the depot to await the return working late at night. This awkward manoeuvre involving holiday and excursion traffic was carried out countless times over the years, nearly always involving a third engine whose job was merely to haul the rake of coaches a short distance over the connection between the two lines at this point. The simplicity of the junction at Netherfield makes it difficult to understand why it was not put back in, for example, in the 1920's when the LNER and LMS were co-operating in the Nottinghamshire area in the building of a joint line of railway to serve the colliery at Bilsthorpe. The lines of rail going off behind the signal box describe an arc around the carriage sidings and effectively upgrade the line between this point and the Midland Station, which can just be glimpsed above the last coach, to four tracks. The distinctive outlines of the train shed at Low Level Station are easily made out above the train, by this date of course no longer entertaining passenger. The residence opposite the signal box was provided for the crossing keeper and is certainly the oldest building in view, probably dating back to the time when the Lincoln line was built.

Photo: R.W. Sheppard

72. Gedling, 1950s. Gedling looking west, showing in the foreground the line leading into the small goods yard, and also the dock adjacent to the down platform. On the up line W.D. 2-8-0 No. 90280 hustles through with a Colwick bound freight train somewhat abbreviated in length. During the 1950s Colwick Shed found employment for large numbers of these engines, and worked them on some of the longer trips, to Peterborough, March, Hull, and down the GN/LNWR Joint line towards Northampton, as well as more locally to the Ilkeston area with wagons of iron ore from the Vale of Belvoir. Somewhere out of sight in the distance was Gedling Colliery Platform, used many years ago by the miners special trains, known as "Paddy Mails" which ran return journeys three times a day at shift change time, and comprising a rake of coaches which had a most certainly seen better days.

Photo: Author's collection

73. Mapperley, 31st July 1957. With steam to spare class 04/8 No. 63657 drifts down the grade between Arno Vale and Mapperley Tunnel with the vital commodity that this line carried throughout its life. The rural aspect belies the fact that the centre of Nottingham is only 3 miles distant.

74. Mapperley Tunnel, August 1955. Black smoke fills the air confirming the effort put in by this modest locomotive bringing 10 coaches up the grade from Mapperley Tunnel towards the summit at Arno Vale. Class 4F No. 43837 proudly displays express headlamps with the Saturdays only Summer train from Skegness to Kings Norton, which ran by the way of Colwick North Junction, Egginton Junction and Burton-on-Trent. *Photo: J.R. Bonser*

75. Mapperley Tunnel, 12 August 1959. Due to old mine workings the section of line between Basford and Colwick was from time to time plagued by subsidence, which sometimes had the effect of distorting the formation and often rendered the gradient chart to nothing more than an approximate guide rather than an accurate record. At other times Mapperley Tunnel suffered and no matter in what way the line was affected the inevitable result was the imposition of a speed limit and therefore the slowing up of traffic flow on the back line was referred to.

On the 23rd of January 1925 part of the tunnel roof collapsed and the line east of Daybrook could not be used for several weeks. Again in the late 1950's colliery subsidence wreaked havoc on the crown of the tunnel which had to be shored up with timber supports, clearly visible in this illustration of the eastern exit. The extent of repairs required viewed in the light of the existence of an alternative route between Basford North and Colwick via Carrington with sufficient spare capacity to cope with the additional traffic militated towards the closure of the line announced to be effective from the 4th of April 1960.

Excursions to the East Coast Resorts were common place when the line was in regular use, these originating from places such as Burton-on-Trent, Pinxton, Pleasley and the many stations serving the mining villages, but the one train which will always be identified with this route was the Summer Saturdays train timetabled during the 1950's to run from King's Norton (Birmingham) to Skegness, which train brought an LMS engine without fail. Drifting down hill through the deep cutting to the east of the tunnel this particular train is headed by Stanier class 5 No. 45024. *Photo: C.A. Hill*

76. (Bottom left) Daybrook, n.d. Directly east of Daybrook Station the GN Line climbed towards Arno Vale Summit and crossed the main Nottingham to Mansfield Road by means of this unusual bridge. This view is looking north and shows the brick arches which separated pedestrians from road traffic at this point and also the advantage taken by bill posters of the large expanse of blue brick wall. Dixon and Parker clearly intended to outdo everyone else in the advertising stakes but strangely enough anyone wishing to purchase one of their doubtless splendid cycle suits would have to turn round and pedal the 3 miles or so back into the city or alternatively having gone through the bridge they could turn left into the station approach and then catch the train. The horse drawn dray seems to be heading along Mansfield Road beyond the bridge perhaps making its way to the Home Brewery premises no more than half a mile away. In later years the bridge was widened to accommodate ever increasing traffic on Mansfield Road, but now the entire scene has changed and some detective work would be required to establish that a railway ever existed at this point. A few yards to the East of this underbridge the Nottingham Suburban Line once went off to the South and in so doing afforded a useful if steeply graded cut off for the Leen Valley trains saving the detour via Gedling. *Photo: Author's collection*

OUR GUINEA CYCLE SUITS
DIXON & PARKER

77. Daybrook, c.1955. The head code proclaims that this is an ordinary passenger train, a fact also indicated by the number and type of coaches. It is in truth one of those peculiar trains where the main purpose seems to have been to give Gedling some kind of service. It started at Basford North and rather than take the direct route to Nottingham Victoria it dived under the GC Main Line near Bagthorpe Junction, paused at Daybrook before continuing its journey "round the back" as it was called via Gedling and the west curve at Colwick thus strangely enough entering Nottingham Victoria from the south. The train hauled by Class J39 No. 64823 is seen near the summit of the line at Arno Vale and will soon be running on favourable gradients towards Mapperley Tunnel. There used to exist a signal box at Arno Vale and from either side trains struggled up the incline predominantly laden eastbound and unladen westbound, although of course there were exceptions to this basic rule. For example coal would be taken from Colwick Yards to Stanton Iron Works, whilst iron stone would be taken westbound to Stanton near Ilkeston or alternatively to Bestwood Iron Works. Corresponding empty workings of iron ore wagons provide an example of empty wagon workings towards Colwick.

Although the pattern of things changed considerably with the opening of the Great Central Railway and the connections at Bagthorpe Junction and Bulwell, it is interesting to study the passage of trains at this summit taken from records relevant to October 1899. The London and North Western Railway ran up to 12 coal trains daily, admittedly some of them only running as required, their origins being New Hucknall, Beighton, and other locations on the Great Central System north of Kirkby-in-Ashfield. Additionally the same company ran a goods train originating "from beyond Egginton Junction" to its Manvers Street Goods Depot in Nottingham, passing Arno Vale at 4.45am Another fast goods train from Sheffield to Colwick was booked to pass Arno Vale at 11.20pm but not on Saturdays. Going West the same company ran an express goods train from Manvers Street to Liverpool which topped the summit at 8.43pm.

The Great Central Company for its part ran a goods train between Annesley and Colwick but was not the only other pre-grouping company to use the line on a regular basis, for a North Staffordshire Railway engine brought a train load of coal from Alsager past Arno Vale at 4.00am, the engine returning with empties to Alsager passing the same point at 10.30pm, the crew doubtless lodging at Colwick during the day. On the domestic scene GN coal trains originating both on and off its own system, were punctuated by an interesting selection of other workings, not incidentally confined to passenger traffic, although even here a Grantham to Stafford via Radcliffe and Gedling service passed this way at 8.12am

The early hours once more provide an interesting selection of the more unique goods services nearly all of these running Mondays excepted. The fast goods from Kings Cross to Manchester struggled up to the Arno Vale summit due at 12.45am, the train then taking the Pinxton branch as far as Brinsley Junction whence the Manchester area was reached courtesy of the Midland Railway Company over whose lines the GN exercised running powers. At 1.25am a fast goods train from Doncaster to Burton-on-Trent also occupied the down line and just over 2 hours later a through goods train from Colwick to the GN's western extremity at Stafford trundled by. At 4.32 yet another fast goods train from Kings Cross came this way, the destination this time being Stoke-on-Trent with a note indicating that the GN Engine would work throughout. Again this may be presumed to be a lodging turn because the balancing working passed Arno Vale at 1.06am. No wonder photographs do not appear of these goods trains but has anyone ever photographed a GN loco resting on Stoke's shed between duties, I wonder? Empties from Colwick to Manchester came by at 6.45 followed by a series of trains which by comparison were unremarkable until the empty milk vans returning from Kings Cross to Tutbury graced the scene at 11.10am. Unlike many other companies the Great Northern Railway did not attach milk traffic to the tail of passenger workings but rather chose to run them as special trains in their own right, and in so doing built up a respectable trade in the Staffordshire area.

On the up line once more the more important goods trains ran during the hours of darkness and thus to a large extent went unobserved, the star performers being the two fast goods trains from Manchester to London, both dashing past the signalman at Arno Vale when he was probably thinking that all decent folk should be asleep in their beds. In the evening once the 9 o'clock LNW coal train to Colwick had gone by the road was cleared for the fast goods train from Burton-on-Trent to Carlton Fields which came by at 9.15 carrying important traffic which would be sorted out for various destinations countrywide. At 9.30 the last passenger train of the day between Stafford and Nottingham approached from the Daybrook direction followed only 5 minutes later by a fast goods train from Derby to Kings Cross. The final two important trains of the day on the up line were identical in that they both originated at Egginton Junction and carried milk only for London. These of course ran with the priority of any goods train carrying perishable traffic, namely as express goods. To summarise, the up line carried 110 booked trains plus 10 others which ran when required. In the down direction the total was 106 plus 9 which ran in accordance with the demands of traffic, these between one midnight and the next.

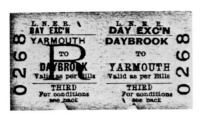

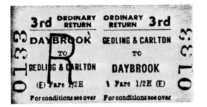

78. Daybrook, July 1951. Daybrook for Arnold, so reads the station name board at the west end of the Up platform which houses the principal station buildings. The architectural style here was typical of many locations on the GN Derbyshire Lines, Awsworth and Pinxton being two examples, with distinctive steep gables edged with decorative barge boards reminiscent of the same company's signal boxes. The buildings were of red brick with grey slate roof and incorporated both ladies and general waiting rooms as well as booking and station master's office and other usual facilities expected at a suburban station. The more distant part of the buildings are two storey and comprise the residence for the station master. The wrought iron footbridge illuminated by two sentry like oil lamps has an attractive appearance whose graceful low arc should appeal to modellers. Standing astride the bottom foot step on each platform are wooden notice boards insisting that "passengers must cross by this bridge" and as if to reinforce the command the outline of a hand with a pointed finger leaves the matter in no doubt. More spartan buildings were provided on the Down line from which doubtless a minority of passengers commenced their journey from this station. On the Up platform a solitary flat barrow lies apparently redundant. The connection from the Up line into the goods yard is seen at bottom right, the latter being partly occupied by timber bodied wagons bearing some evidence of former private ownership. Unused space at this station gave the opportunity in the Second World War for the army mail destined for forces serving in the Middle East to be sorted here and, as with

London Road Low Level, a special train was put on to convey this important cargo. Daybrook signal box is some distance behind the camera but the up starter is seen beyond the footbridge, beyond which on the north side of the line Daybrook Junction signal box stood until 1934. At the date of this photograph the junction with the Nottingham Suburban Railway was a single line connection with the down line, access to which was obtained first by means of setting back over the station cross over and then travelling wrong line for a short distance as far as the ground frame. In earlier years a signal gantry spanning both main lines could be seen approximately where the up starting signal appears, vertical timbers passing through the cross bar and somersault type signals being mounted at either end of these. The upper arms were slightly higher than the signal arms shown on this photograph but the lower arms would have been visible under the arc of the footbridge, the latter of course being the cause of the signals being of the repeater type, yet another modeller's delight no doubt. The odd thing about the signal arms which were in use when the connection to the Suburban Railway was a normal flat double track junction, was that they were both mounted at the same level thus appearing to give neither line distinction of being the more important of the two although the majority of the traffic went straight ahead towards Colwick. The double line junction was in use until February 1930 when the junction at this point was altered to converge into a single track.

Photo: D. Thompson

79. (Right) Leen Valley Jn, 11th April 1964. Pale sunlight of a spring day leaves us in no doubt as to the location of this GN type signal box with its typical ornate barge boarding and still at this late date retaining its double finial, not only on the main roof but additionally to a smaller scale on the outbuilding. Here, the signalman controlled traffic to and from the vital lines serving the collieries of the Leen Valley and those further afield out as far as Pleasley and Shirebrook, where it joined the main line to Derby. Until the collapse of Mapperley Tunnel in 1960, nearly all the goods and mineral traffic bound for Colwick Yards came this way, as often as not hauled by an eight coupled locomotive. In those far off days before the railway companies were grouped into the big four in 1923, the Ivatt "Long Toms", 0-8-0 tender locomotives, were used alongside the tank version counterparts which became Class R1 on the LNER. The LNWR 0-8-0 tender engines were also much in evidence but by nationalisation in 1948 the several varieties of Class 04 2-8-0 together with the ex War Department "Austerities" of like wheel arrangement, provided the mainstay for coal traffic. By the time this photograph was taken, very few ex LNER types survived at Colwick, which had instead acquired the Stanier 8Fs. Almost inevitably the site is now a housing estate whose residents would search in vain for any trace of the railway.

Photo: M.S. Castledine

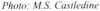

80. Colwick. The small signal box at Netherfield Lane controlled a level crossing about mid-way along the spur from Netherfield Station to Colwick North Junction, the line forming the Western leg of the triangle there. Although displaying many of the characteristics of a typical GNR signal box it is looking rather shabby at this stage of its life.   *Photo: D. Thompson*

81. Basford North, 7th May 1955. Around Nottinghamshire the MR got in first and so claimed for itself the easier routes running mainly along river valleys. Later arrivals on the scene required to build more in the way of cuttings tunnels and often embankments and bridges, a situation well depicted in this unusual but charming view to the west of Basford North Station. Class J6 No. 64215 has charge of Grantham to Derby stopping train, a task often entrusted to this type of locomotive. The distinctive signalling products of the two pre-grouping companies are conveniently placed to complete the picture.   *Photo: J. Cupit*

82. Bulwell Forest, 18th June 1959. As the evening shadows lengthen another train load of coal bound for Colwick Yards is wheeled past the all timber signal box at 8.30pm. The class 04 locomotive No. 63758 has a round topped boiler and formed part 7 in the class grouping. Sixteen ton capacity wagons of metal construction make up the majority of the train, the entire scene being of neat appearance.   *Photo: P.J. Lynch*

83. Bulwell Forest, c.1931. Bulwell Forest was the first station along the GNR Leen valley branch although not every train would call here on its way to Newstead or Shirebrook, possibly because it retained a fairly rural setting right up to the time when local passenger services were taken off on 5th September 1931. Nearby was, and still is, a municipal golf course but the only other premises of note belonged to William Wrigley & Sons, wagon repairers and builders, adjacent to the up line. Shortly after cessation of local stopping trains, Nottingham Corporation put up a large housing estate in the vicinity, too late in the day for their tenants to make use of the infrequent services offered, although by that time buses had claimed for themselves people wishing to travel to the city centre. Later still, from about 1960 onwards, many acres of land belonging to the Duke of St. Alban's Trustees have been sold for development on a massive scale, including the Rise Park and Top Valley Estates at Bestwood. The Leen Valley route carried a basic service comprising nine down and eight up trains, with two extras on Saturdays, one being a down only late night affair returning revellers to Sutton-in-Ashfield. However, only four plus one on Saturdays came via Daybrook, the others using the direct line from Victoria to Bulwell Common, by-passing Bulwell Forest in the process. In this view, non-existant passengers are enjoined to cross the line only by the bridge to catch the Nottingham bound train. Seats appear to be at a premium, but, on a cold day, there is no doubt it was possible to keep warm by one of the fires which cheered both the Ladies and the General Waiting Rooms forming part of the timber building to the right of the picture. The presence of wooden platforms here may have been due to mining subsidence and not for any economic reason.   *Photo: D. Thompson*

84. Bulwell Forest, 19th September 1959. Despite having been closed to passenger trains for the best part of thirty years Bulwell Forest looks commendably tidy as Push and Pull fitted LMS 2-6-2T No. 41320, of Wellingborough shed and complete with express headlamps, takes charge of the Railway Correspondence & Travel Society railtour. In this view looking south the train passes the low timber platform having just cleared the GNR style home signal. Just to the north of the station the sidings lead off on the east side of the line into the wagon repair works of William Wrigley & Sons which can be seen to be left of the picture. This company was involved in building metal bodied wagons for BR in the 1950s but is best remembered for carrying out repairs to goods rolling stock, predominantly mineral wagons. Towards the end of the steam era, some locomotives were brought here to be cut up, including exLMS rebuilt Patriots and moguls of Class K1. Today the scene is changed beyond all recognition and the station and wagon works site has been redeveloped as a large supermarket with adjacent residential properties.
     Photo: T.G. Hepburn/Author's collection

85. Basford North, 11th April 1964. Looking West from the station footbridge a named class B1 No. 61003 *Gazelle* blows off furiously and deafens three spectators as it cuts a dash through the haze on an early morning parcels train to Nottingham from Derby Friargate.   *Photo: M.S. Castledine*

86. Basford North, c.1959. Definitely a stranger in the camp. These were the engines which infuriated loco spotters for they were devoid of smoke box number plates and if you stuck your head out of the carriage window to see a Super D coming along the adjacent track you would be hard pressed to get its identification. They were a London and North Western design improved upon in later years which in turn meant that they had long lives. Despite this they very rarely strayed from their parent system. Granted that Nottingham's link with the London and North Western Railway was via Market Harborough to Northampton, it would be acceptable though quite rare to see a Northampton Super D earning its keep but this particular specimen with its tender cab hailed from Bescot (Walsall) and the reason for its appearance as late as 1959 on a braked good train defies explanation. No. 49407 may well have been the last of its type to reach the Nottingham area as it recreates a spectacle by then 30 years out of date.   *Photo: C.A. Hill*

87. Bulwell Common, 7th May 1955.
Running tender first class 04 No. 63657 has just re-started from a signal check on the 1 in 75 gradient between Basford North and Bulwell Common South Junction with a train destined for the Leen Valley Line. An all out effort was required by engine and crew to prevent the weight of the train winning the battle against the severe gradient, exacerbated by the sharp curve, but for more years than one cares to say Colwick men worked with these engines and knew how to get the best from them. Needless to say the load was hauled up the incline and once the gradient eased at Bulwell Common South, the engine strode away in confident style. Indicative of the curving approach at this point, the position of the signals on the opposite side of the line to normal will be noted.
Photo: E.C.N. Haywood

88. Basford North, 1st October 1959.
Perhaps the strangest train service in the local timetable around this time was that of the line through Gedling. Some six months before it finally expired class A5 No. 69825 sets off from Basford North in determined style with the 4.15pm "round the back". At least six vehicles in tow including some main line stock, the driver will call at Daybrook, Gedling and Netherfield along this indirect route before coming to rest in Victoria Station facing north. To the left of the scene is the substantial goods shed provided to cater for the many and varied manufacturing industries hereabouts, the exit of the main line being protected by a bank of five miniature arms on a single lattice post. To the right of the signal box the west to north connection with Bulwell Common used for example by the Burton-on-Trent to York beer train can be glimpsed. *Photo: Author's collection*

89. Basford North, c.1966. The station has been closed to passengers for about two years, although facilities for goods will linger on until 1967. The station buildings are partially obscured from view by the tremendous exhaust but the twisted chimney stacks give the location away. There was a daily oil train working at this time to Colwick which brought a Birkenhead class 9F into the area. The return working of empties was a late afternoon turn, on this occasion worked by one of the ex-Crosti boilered specimens of most distinctive appearance. Although fitted with a standard boiler the external appearance of the 10 locomotives concerned was not altered significantly in rebuilding, but there is no doubt that they had a distinctly continental look about them. Following rebuilding they eventually became scattered amongst different sheds in the north west of the country with the result that they were widely travelled and often photographed. This photograph by Don Beecroft must surely rank as one of the best. The continental feel is enhanced by the shape of the vehicles which make up the train load.
Photo: D.H. Beecroft

90. Colwick Shed GN, c.1930. For many reasons it was not easy to photograph Colwick depot in such a manner as would give an impression of its size and layout. Fortunately, an aerial picture has survived showing the offices and mess rooms in the foreground which made any unofficial visit to the shed a risky business. The earliest buildings dating from 1876 are the four roads under the double pitched roof on the right, but due to the rapid expansion of the coalfield and the further development of lines by the GNR some six years later, the taller pitched roof building was provided for the repair of engines and at the same time the further eight road shed to its left was brought into use. Even this was inadequate, so before the turn of the century the final four roads on the left adjacent to the wagon repair shops were added. Major improvements were effected in the 1930s by the LNER with the aid of government loans, including the provision of a larger turntable, better facilities for engine disposal and the mechanical coaling stage, for at this time more than two hundred engines were based at Colwick. Numbers began to decline in later years after 1960 leading to eventual closure and transfer of the remaining traffic to former MR lines, so a survey of the locomotive allocation in August 1950 in busier times follows. This discloses ten B1s, four B17s lingering on before being transferred to East Anglia, their places being taken by more B1s, twelve K2s – by then ageing but still capable of giving a good account of themselves – six K3s, popular for excursions and express goods work, shared with class J39 of which no less than twenty five worked from Colwick. Two elderly four coupled tender engines eked out their last days, one of which is reputed to have hauled a three coach passenger train the 3 miles or so uphill from Mansfield Central to Sutton-in-Ashfield without stopping but taking 20 minutes to complete the journey! Pre-grouping six coupled tender engines of GNR origin were still plentiful, comprising four each of classes J1 and J2, no less than eighteen J5s – nearly the entire class, and sixteen of the very useful J6 class. Odd man out was ex GCR class J11 No. 64301. Fifteen of the ubiquitous GCR type 04s, many of them reboilered, were outnumbered by the Austerity 2-8-0s built during the second world war. Forty four of these unsung workhorses were on the strength, and despite being unpopular in many quarters, Colwick men managed to get the best from them. Finally, shunting was in the hands of fifteen saddle tanks of class J52 assisted by two N5s of GCR design and six J50s. Four class N2 passenger tanks found work on the Mansfield line but did not reign long and the eleven handsome A5 engines were held in better esteem. Not even one diesel shunter was to be found in this total of 199 engines.

Photo: courtesy Nottingham Central Library

91. Colwick, c.1928. Following the 1923 grouping the LNER was not slow to break down the barriers of the old companies at least as far as locomotive use was concerned. For years Colwick drivers had shared the lines around Nottingham with their colleagues from GCR establishments and many opportunities must have arisen to examine and compare each others engines. The impoverished LNER was able to buy up cheaply a large number of GCR designed 2-8-0s government surplus after the Great War, and to spread them widely around its territory. Colwick received some of these, and took to them well, so it is not surprising to find other GCR types on shed. No. 6131 looks at home outside the eight road shed which was built in 1882. The taller building behind is the repair and lifting shop erected at the same time signifying Colwick's status as a main depot equipped to carry out heavy overhauls not requiring a visit to works. To enable Colwick to fulfil its repair and maintenance duties as the main shed in the group, which meant that it covered engines from Leicester and Annesley as well as its own, it was provided with a substantial amount of equipment, including sheer legs in the yard enabling the removal of wheels from an engine, a wheel drop and pit on number one road of the Old shed, and a 36 ton capacity overhead crane in the Erecting Shop, which, in common with the Fitters Shop had full bench facilities. Senior positions on the maintenance side were Mechanical Chargeman and Boiler Chargeman, one of each on three shifts, six men in total, and they supervised some fifty or so fitters, 8 boilersmiths, 2 skilled machinists, 2 blacksmiths and strikers, 2 coppersmiths and 4 others expert in retubing a boiler. One man had the unpleasant job of repairing brick arches all to himself, but no doubt he enlisted help from some junior grades. Each shift required two gangs of boiler washers to keep the engines in good order and available for rostering. The blacksmith's shop contained two furnaces with anvils and a steam hammer, whilst the machine shop was equipped with four lathes and one adapted for boring axle boxes, a further wheel lathe in constant use, a radial drill and other machines for drilling and shaping. Thus provided with machines and skilled labour, Colwick undertook much more than day to day maintenance. Piston and valve examinations were carried out, side rods and bushes were within its jurisdiction, wheel turning and routine mileage boiler examinations, as well as investigating failures all kept the place a hive of activity, as well as cutting down the number of engines which had to be sent to main works for repair. However, when the boiler condition became unacceptable, or it was at the end of its useful life, or the engine mileage reached about a hundred thousand in the case of the goods locomotives, a visit to Gorton or Doncaster Works was inevitable.

Photo: Author's collection

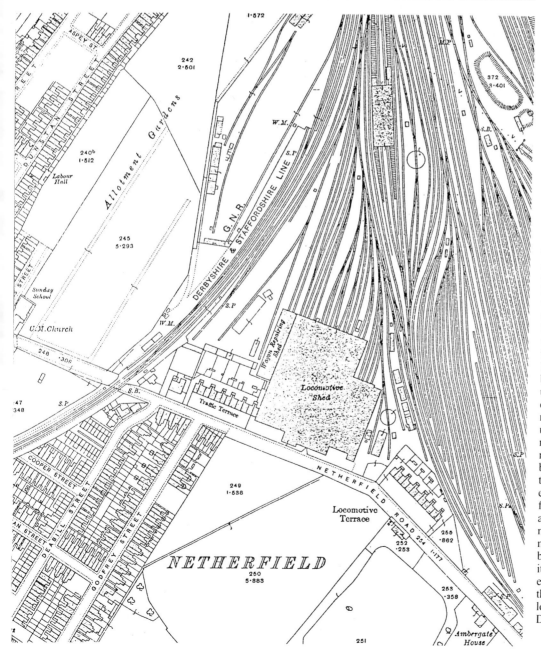

92. Colwick Shed, c.1955. Definitely not an everyday sight at Colwick, No. 60029 *Woodcock* is indeed a rare bird. The coding of 38A gave Colwick the status of being a parent shed, to which locomotives allocated to other sheds in the group were often sent for main examinations. Therefore when the Gresley Pacifics were based at Leicester (38C) they were no strangers, but of course they were not of the stream-lined variety. Pondering the photograph it was conjectured that the locomotive may have failed at Grantham on the main line and been sent to Colwick which was geographically speaking the nearest parent shed. Alternatively it is well known that at certain times in its history Kings Cross shed has been hard pressed to find repair staff and hence the locomotive could have been sent to Colwick as a deliberate move to speed up its return to traffic. The real reason was only discovered on speaking with Sid Checkley, a long serving member of the mechanical engineering staff and a person of countless recollections from his days spent there. It transpires that *Woodcock* had worked north with an excursion train from Marylebone to Doncaster and had to be taken off the train at Nottingham on the return leg due to brake problems in that the vacuum brake kept leaking on. A B1 was substituted and *Woodcock* was sent to Colwick to be examined. By all accounts the fault was quickly traced and this photograph was taken "just for the record" before the engine was sent home.

Photo: S. Checkley

93. Colwick Shed GN, 7th June 1931. A veritable army of six coupled tender engines was housed at Colwick during the inter-war years for use on a variety of turns ranging from shunting the adjacent yards, working mineral trains to and from the pits, covering the rush hour local passenger duties and even tackling successfully the cheap excursion trains to the east coast resorts. One such engine Class J3 No. 4141, scrapped only two years after this photograph was taken, poses alongside the raised coalstage. Despite the provision of a concrete cenotaph coaler about 1933, with such a large allocation Colwick retained the older appartus in use as well. Bays were provided along the side elevation from which coal was fed into waiting tenders by means of chutes, one of which is visible on the left. Up to two hundred engines each day were coaled, and, if one assumes an average of five tons each, some idea of the magnitude of the task and its continuous nature can be perceived. One thousand tons would be two full trainloads of coal! Moreover, the clerical staff had the job of accounting for every ton of coal received and used.

Photo: Author's collection

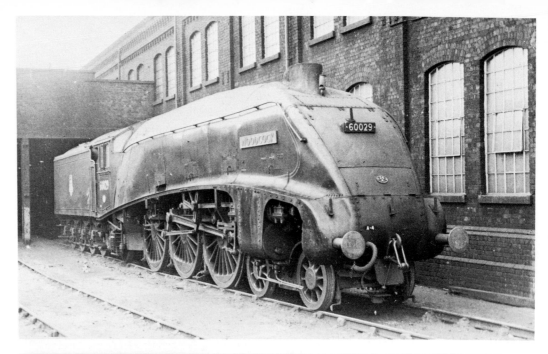

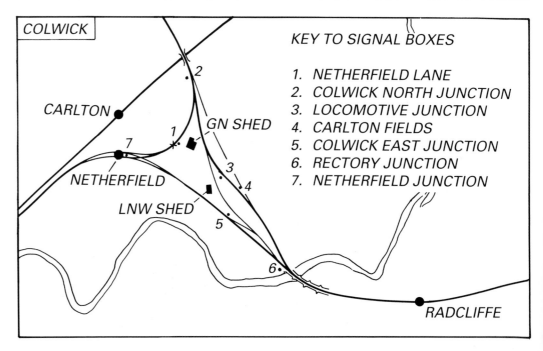

COLWICK

KEY TO SIGNAL BOXES

1. NETHERFIELD LANE
2. COLWICK NORTH JUNCTION
3. LOCOMOTIVE JUNCTION
4. CARLTON FIELDS
5. COLWICK EAST JUNCTION
6. RECTORY JUNCTION
7. NETHERFIELD JUNCTION

CARLTON

GN SHED

NETHERFIELD

LNW SHED

RADCLIFFE

94. Colwick (LNW), c.1922. LNWR 0-8-0 No. 2201 stands outside the shed waiting its next call for duty. These locomotives along with the six coupled DX goods as they were known formed the mainstay of the allocation to the depot, which concerned itself almost exclusively with the movement of coal firstly from the colliery to the adjacent yards, then by the trainload to Willesden via Northampton. Out of sight beyond the water tower was the turntable. Staff accommodation was carefully sought out and satisfied by the provision of 37 cottages in two adjacent rows and appropriately called London and North Western Terrace. Some of these dwellings can be seen on the right of the picture, and they lasted well beyond closure of the shed, and were occupied until relatively recent times. The front of these houses looked out towards the depot, but there was precious little ground to the rear for garden use. However, on the south side of the engine shed an area of about one and a half acres was set aside for use as allotments, access being by means of a cinder track.

Photo: Author's collection

95. Colwick (LNW), 7 June 1931. Having secured for itself a respectable share of the local coal traffic entirely by means of running powers over lines of other railway companies, the LNWR did at least build its own engine shed which it established adjacent to Colwick Sidings. In fact it probably over catered for its needs by erecting an eight road northlight type building of stark appearance. Here the six and eight coupled tender engines were looked after, and, amongst other repairs performed, the driving wheels of locomotives could be removed for attention. Nottingham (Midland) shed had no wheeldrop facility, but after the 1923 grouping of railways with the LNWR and MR coming together as part of the LMS it was convenient for engines to be sent out to Colwick for such matters until that shed closed in December 1932. The wheeldrops were then salvaged and then removed to Nottingham. In this view LMS Compound No. 928 awaits the return of its rear driving wheels on the dead end road at the west side of the shed.

Photo: Author's collection

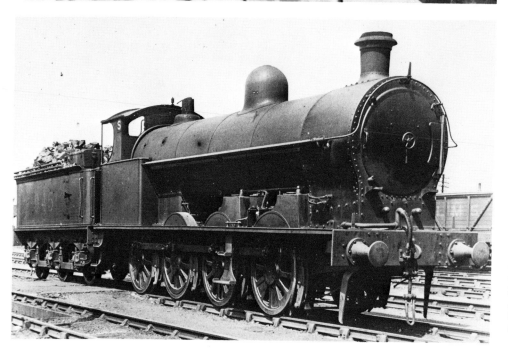

96. Colwick (LNW), c.1925. Bowen-Cooke's superheated heavy goods design No. 9451 stands outside the shed on what seems a pleasant day facing the right way to be rostered to work south via the GN/LNWR Joint line. Observe the metal plate on the side of the cab displaying a white letter S, a practice peculiar to the LNWR, even though this view was taken in early LMS days. This symbol was carried by a locomotive either recently built or fresh from overhaul at Crewe Works and signifies that No. 9451 was in supreme condition. On the extreme left of the picture the footbridge may be seen straddling the single line entrance to the shed, and it would have made an excellent vantage point from which to photograph the depot given certain light conditions as the camera would have been pointing due south. A record dated October 1899 shows the LNWR operating eleven mineral and two goods trains into Colwick Yards daily, the latter coming from Burton-on-Trent and Sheffield respectively. After closure the shed stood for many years in a forlorn state as a reminder of a company which somehow seemed alien to Nottingham.

Photo: Author's collection

97. Bingham Road, n.d. The station here was in a fairly rural setting close by the main road from Nottingham to Grantham and stood little chance of competing for passenger trade with the more centrally located Bingham Station with its frequent service along the Grantham Line which also took Nottingham-bound passengers right to the heart of the city whereas from Bingham Road, certainly at the time this photograph was taken, the destination would be London Road Low Level Station. It would be interesting to know how many tickets were sold in the space of a week. The line here was constructed jointly by the LNWR and the GNR, the latter company making good use of it by fetching the iron ore, mined in east Leicestershire, and taking it by the train load to the Stanton Iron Works at Ilkeston. The former company on the other hand took its full loads in the opposite direction and this was indeed an important artery used by the LNWR for the flow of coal traffic and in its hey day was well enough occupied with various types of mineral trains and the corresponding return flow of empty wagons so that it is perhaps as well that the passenger service was not developed to any great degree. A local train of typically light formation pauses hopefully for business. Engine No. 219 enjoyed a long and useful life having been much rebuilt over the years including the provision of a belpaire boiler.

Photo: Author's collection

98. Bingham Road, c.1950. A passenger timetable for 1939 provides four trains to Nottingham and only five each day from the near side platform in the opposite direction. With that frequency of service and being a little way out of Bingham itself it is difficult to imagine people in the waiting room fighting to find a seat. The station closed its doors finally in July 1951.

Photo: D. Thompson

The Nottingham Suburban Railway

Although little over 3½ miles in length the Nottingham Suburban Railway has an interesting if chequered career. This chapter does not set out to be a definitive history of the line, rather it is a brief introduction to and commentary upon it. For those concerned to know more an excellent thoroughly researched and detailed article appeared under the authorship of John Marshall in the *British Railway Journal* issue No. 14, which is unreservedly commended to the reader.

It is suggested that there were two main reasons why the line was proposed by a group of local business men including Robert Mellors, a benefactor of the city and then chairman of the Nottingham Patent Brick Company. Firstly the hilly area to the North East of the city contained considerable deposits of clay, a basic necessity for making bricks, which in the 1880's were needed in large quantities for the extensive developments that were taking place throughout the country. Prior to the building of the line, the possibility of a direct rail access to serve these brickworks had seemed very remote and in that respect the building of the Suburban line was in the nature of a self-help exercise. It was of course inevitable that the line would have to make a connection with one or other of the major pre-grouping railway companies and it soon became clear that the GNR would be the one most likely to be receptive to the scheme. That company's station was in London Road, as has been indicated, not particularly convenient to the developing city, and all train services which that company operated to the north and west of Nottingham were obliged to make the initial part of the journey via Netherfield, hence initially in the wrong direction so that by the time the train had clocked up seven miles or more it had still got no further than Daybrook, a distance of slightly over three miles as the crow flies. Robert Mellors and his colleagues saw the opportunity to attract the GNR Company to its proposals by making connections with that company's lines, at both ends of the new line, thus providing a fairly direct route to the north and to the west of Nottingham, the burden of stiff gradients being out-weighed by the reduced mileage and the likelihood of a clear run out to Daybrook as opposed to being delayed by the important and heavy flow of coal traffic between there and Colwick.

So it was that a Bill was laid before Parliament in the 1886 session supported strongly by local trades organisations, the proprietors of the Nottingham Brick Company, and indeed the Nottingham Corporation itself. With such initial support which included financial grants, the GNR Company was approached with confidence, this resulted in the chairman and some of the directors of that established company visiting the area through which the new line would run, the visit being made some six months before the Bill became an Act of Parliament. That the GNR Company was interested may be gauged by the fact that the new company was empowered to make the required connections at each end of its new line and indeed to enter into working agreements which covered the supply of rolling stock, machinery and even staff to work on the line.

Edward Parry then 42 years of age, previously the Nottinghamshire County Surveyor, and also a director of the Brick Company was appointed engineer to the NSR Company and under his supervision the line was built between June 1887 and November 1889 at a cost of £262,500, not surprisingly in view of the terrain, in excess of Edward Parry's estimate of £194,000. At the southern end the original plans for the connection to the GNR had been amended, eventually giving way to a flying junction so as not to interrupt any of the traffic on the line between Nottingham and Grantham. The gradients were awkward here, the down line being at 1 in 49 whereas the longer up line which passed over the GNR line by means of a bow string girder bridge on a ruling gradient of 1 in 50. Indeed 1 in 50 was the measure of the adverse incline faced by a northbound train most of the way to the summit of the line just prior to the 2¼ mile post. From there the line fell through Sherwood Tunnel and station, then through Ashwell's Tunnel towards Daybrook Junction, generally on a ruling gradient of 1 in 70 but with about ¼ of a mile of level track approaching Daybrook. The line was double track throughout with neat but modest stations at Thorneywood, St. Ann's Well and Sherwood, only the last named not being provided with a goods yard and shed. Earth works were heavy with bridges, some entirely constructed of brick, others with girders supported on substantial masonry piers, accompanying deep cuttings and high embankments. All of this says nothing of four tunnels at Sneinton, Thorneywood, Sherwood and Ashwells comprising more than eleven hundred yards of boring.

Two brickworks were connected to the line in the vicinity of Thorneywood whilst the established works at Mapperley belonging to the Nottingham Patent Brick Company fed into the line, north of Sherwood Station by means of a steep incline. It should not be forgotten that the last named company supplied a substantial number of bricks for use in building the line itself, doubtless to its own advantage.

The 2nd December 1889 was fixed for the commencement of passenger services and on that day the first train left London Road Station for Daybrook but this was not without incident, because the contractor Mr Edwards claimed that he still had possession of the line and appointed an agent who apparently attempted to prevent that first train from making progress beyond Trent Lane Junction. From now until 1900 the line enjoyed its hey-day and was certainly at its busiest. The trams had not yet arrived on the scene, let alone the motor car, and for just over 10 years the line was the direct route to the city which it set out to be. In 1890 the Leen Valley Line of course terminated at Newstead and four trains serving that line ran via Sherwood with at least five others going to Daybrook or Basford. In addition to this, from the beginning of 1893 there came a cuckoo into the nest, for the Manchester, Sheffield and Lincolnshire Railway had pushed its line south to make an end on junction with the Leen Valley Line at Newstead, the very line which was to be extended at the end of the last century and thus signal for the Nottingham Suburban Railway the start of its decline. The MS&L ran six week day trains in each direction from Sheffield to London Road Station in Nottingham via Chesterfield, Newstead and Thorneywood, surely one of the strangest routes ever to be taken by regular passenger services between those cities. The GNR made further use of the line by adding into the schedule an Ilkeston train in each direction on week days, which was extended to and from Derby on Fridays only. Later when the Leen Valley extension line was opened to Skegby in 1898, the Suburban Line was coping with 13 northbound and 15 southbound passenger trains in addition to the six between Nottingham and Sheffield already mentioned.

With the opening of Nottingham Victoria Station in 1900 and only 11 years after itself being opened for traffic, the Suburban Railway at a stroke lost most of its importance and from then on fewer stopping passenger trains used the line on account of the direct route to Basford afforded by the Great Central Line and the Junctions at Bagthorpe. The electric tram appeared in Nottingham in 1901 and one of the first routes in operation was from a point close to Sherwood Station and running past the new Nottingham Victoria. This did not help the cause of passenger trains on the Suburban Line; further nails were driven into its coffin with additional tram services along the Wells Road and later along Carlton Road, adjacent to Thorneywood Station. Although several trains used the Suburban Line, some of them entering Nottingham Victoria from the north and then departing via Weekday Cross and Trent Lane without reversal, not all of them served the three stations, often being first stop Daybrook. The photograph produced in this book relates to the period prior to the first world war and shows one of only three southbound stopping trains about to call at Thorneywood, but evidently to no advantage. Small wonder then that on 13th July 1916, partly as a war time measure, the three stations were closed and thereafter in terms of passenger services the line was merely a short cut, until the end came for the Leen Valley Trains in 1931.

Goods traffic on the Suburban Railway was generated by three short branches to brickworks, two of them being at the top of ropeworked inclines, together with local traffic received at and despatched from goods yards at Thorneywood and St. Ann's Well. No records have been consulted relating to timetabled workings of goods trains along the line, but it may be supposed that in the years prior to 1914, there would be two daily trips along the line to clear the goods yards of general merchandise. Much of the traffic would doubtless be to or from the brickworks which had their own direct connections and would therefore account for several wagon loads each day. During the same period the business at St. Ann's Well may have been somewhat sparse because it was not located in a heavily industrialised part of the city. On the other hand Thorneywood found itself somewhat nearer to the factories and markets but even so it probably had a small turnover on account of its geographical proximity to the warehouses of the LNWR at Manvers Street and the GNR at London Road.

In the years after the first world war what traffic there was declined to such an extent that a pick-up goods train running twice or perhaps three times per week was sufficient to cope with the residue. In this respect road transport had made great advances at the expense of the railway. The line did however come into its own for a few days in January 1925, following a fall in the roof of Mapperley Tunnel effectively isolating Colwick yards from much of the coal traffic which kept it going. Obviously some trains were capable of being diverted through Nottingham Victoria Station via the junctions at Bagthorpe and Bulwell Common, but line capacity meant that for a few days traffic was diverted to run via Sherwood and Nottingham Low Level yard where a reversal was necessary. There are no reports of any runaways but suffice it to say that the job of working a 30 wagon loose coupled coal train, up a sharp incline of 1 in 70 followed by 2 miles steeper than that down the grade with a severe curve and a main line junction at the bottom of the slope required a certain amount of skill.

The line was visited by a passenger train once more on 16th June 1951, in the shape of an enthusiasts special and some six weeks later it was cleared of all items of rolling stock, many of which had been stored wagons, and was left quietly to decay for three years until the dismantling train arrived in June 1954. It should be said that from 1941 access could not be gained from the Trent Lane end because the line had been damaged during an air raid in May of 1941. There was evidently no haste in dismantling the line for the junction at Daybrook lingered on until early 1957. Today some of the formation has returned to nature but much of it has either been overbuilt or filled in, and is therefore in many places difficult to trace.

99. Trent Lane Junction, n.d. By an Act of 25th June 1886 the Nottingham Suburban Railway was incorporated with powers to build its main line almost three and three quarter miles in length with gradients as steep as 1 in 50 in parts between Trent Lane Junction and Daybrook Junction. Looking west towards the signal box, the double track main line from Nottingham to Grantham on the right is close to the point where it crosses above the much earlier MR line going out to Lincoln. The down line of the Suburban Railway went off in a northerly direction behind the signal box but the GNR insisted that the up line should be positioned so as not to conflict with traffic bound for Nottingham from Colwick, and it was therefore necessary to construct a flying junction, that line being carried on a fall in gradient of 1 in 49 atop the embankment in the left foreground leading to the girder bridge which crosses the MR line before finally making the connection at Trent Lane West Junction. Behind the photographer of course the up line curved round to cross over the Nottingham to Grantham route and joined with the down Suburban Line at the point where both made a further crossing of the MR line to Lincoln. *Photo: Author's collection*

100. Trent Lane Junction, 2nd August 1954. Class N1 No. 69441 takes empty coaches towards Nottingham and approaches Trent Lane Junction at the point where the Nottingham Suburban Line made its rather awkward connection with the Grantham Line in the eastern suburbs of the city. In this vicinity the Grantham Line kept fairly close company with the Midland Railway tracks but already since leaving the station at London Road the former had crossed over the latter resulting in 3 lines on different levels in a very short distance if one counts the Suburban Railway. The down line feeding the Nottingham Suburban climbed away on an embankment partly concealed by the locomotive whilst the up line fell steeply across the girder bridge in view here before curving round behind the photographer aiming towards Trent Lane. *Photo: Author's collection*

101. Daybrook Junction, c.1951. Off to the seaside with a Ragtimer. This photograph was probably taken on a Sunday because the train is running wrong line due to engineering in the vicinity of Daybrook Station. Having just left the last named place, class K2 No. 61749, tender topped with coal, and carrying express head lamps, takes another train load of day trippers to one of their favourite resorts. Although it was originally a double track connection, by this time the junction at Daybrook with the Nottingham Suburban Line, seen in the left foreground, has been singled. The miniature somersault type signal along side the third coach was not there in pre-grouping days as might be expected but was actually erected by the LNER in 1934. The houses in the right background are on Mansfield Road at Daybrook Square. *Photo: Author's collection*

2. Thorneywood, 1910. Afternoon sun [sm]iling benignly on the approaching train [com]prising teak coaches coupled to a bright [gr]een engine makes its contribution to this [de]lightful scene. The 2.08pm from Basford to [No]ttingham Victoria arrives at Thorneywood [be]hind one of Patrick Stirling's 044 tanks No. [?]2 where it will pause for a few seconds before [con]tinuing down the grade through Sneinton [Tu]nnel. Charming though this photograph may [be] it hardly illustrates a hive of activity, for the [se]at is there unused by travellers preferring the [m]unicipal transport from the adjacent Carlton [Ro]ad, and the posture of the station staff is [de]cidedly unhurried. Taking into account the [ne]ed for a fairly extensive goods yard, space was [at] a premium which resulted in the signal box [be]ing placed on the station platform. Out of [si]ght to the right of the box behind the buildings [on] the up platform is the head shunt of the line [le]ading off in a north easterly direction, under [T]horneywood Lane then up the incline to the [b]rickworks. The building on the far right is the [st]ation master's house which fronted to [T]horneywood Lane. Public access to this station [w]as on the down side, there being a passenger [fo]ot bridge between the platforms behind the [p]hotographer, although the step for the use of the [r]ailway employees will be observed on the [p]latform retaining wall.   *Photo: F. Gillford*

103. Thorneywood, 16th June 1951. By 1951 [t]he Suburban Railway route had been severed [n]ear its southern end, and therefore could only be [s]erved from Daybrook Junction. Word was [a]broad that the goods train which ran two or three [t]imes each week was to be taken off and the line [w]ould then be closed. This was sufficient reason [f]or the Railway Correspondence and Travel [S]ociety to organise a four coach special train [w]hich made a memorable foray to Thorneywood [a]nd back a mere six weeks before final closure [c]ame on 1st August 1951. Some twenty years [e]arlier when the Leen Valley trains were finished, [i]t had fallen to an Ivatt class C 12 to work that last [t]rain to Shirebrook via the Nottingham Suburban [R]ailway, the 5.04pm from Nottingham. It was [t]herefore fitting that the same type of locomotive [s]hould be used again in the form of No. 67363, a [w]ell known performer, splendidly turned out for [t]he occasion.   *Photo: Author's collection*

104. Thorneywood, c.1904. This view looking north towards the mouth of Thorneywood Tunnel serves to explain the difficulties of providing and operating a goods yard at this place. The double track main line is rising at a gradient of 1 in 50 and curving towards the tunnel mouth, and it seems that the sidings are also on the same incline. The line is penned in on the west side by housing development with the lattice girder foot bridge giving residents a direct access to Thorneywood Lane, then to Carlton Road, whilst the contours on the east side of the line are such that a substantial retaining wall is required. Usually one of the two lines to the right had to be kept clear to allow access to the brickworks situated on a higher level to the east of Thorneywood Road; there was of course more space on the west side of the running lines, just enough in fact to provide for two loops occupied by the wagons which partly conceal the goods shed building and a further siding on the western edge of the layout beyond the goods shed by the horse drawn carts. If the camera were to be turned to face the opposite way Thorneywood Station would be in the foreground and that itself is penned in by Carlton Road, under which the lines pass.

105. St. Ann's Well, c.1904. Middle of the three stations on the Nottingham Suburban Railway was St. Ann's Well some 3/4 miles from Trent Lane West Junction. This is the view looking north at which point the gradient has temporarily eased to 1 in 200. Public access was via a road constructed at the joint expense of the railway company and the local authority connecting the Wells Road and the down side of the station. The road ran virtually parallel with the line of rail on the westerly side, whilst the space to the east of the station platforms was taken up by a small goods yard, the brick shed being just visible behind the up line platform buildings. The base of the Nottingham bound platform is the only one of the six platforms on the Suburban line to be constructed entirely of timber. If this photograph is compared with those showing Thorneywood and Sherwood Stations, the degree of standardisation becomes obvious.

106. Sherwood. A closer look at the facilities available at Sherwood is afforded in this view from track level between the platform faces, highlighting the standard treatment of scalloped fretwork applied to the canopies, and giving prominence to the elliptical footbridge by Andrew Handyside & Co supplied to the stations on the Suburban line.

107. Sherwood, c.1904. Once again, another view at track level showing the solidly engineered route of the Suburban line, particularly the road overbridge. Another feature captured, intentionally or otherwise, is the reverse side of the somersault signals, familiar to Great Northern Railway students.

108. Bulwell Common, 13th July 1959. Although the two trains appear to be running neck and neck it isn't a race because precedence has been given to the down South Yorkshireman 4.50pm ex-Marylebone, a 10 coach train of which 3 will be dropped at Sheffield to proceed after Penistone via the ex-Lancashire and Yorkshire route to Huddersfield behind a Low Moor Black 5. Class B1 No. 61383 attacks the climb to Kirkby dashing through the station sometime after seven in the evening and passes another of the line's better known trains which will then follow it. This latter headed by York based B16 No. 61434, a rebuilt variety, is the much lamented Burton-on-Trent to York beer train, worked by York shed and frequently entrusted to this ex-Northeastern Railway design. When one thinks of the obvious direct route via Chesterfield Midland linking the two places one has to conclude that the LNER and later the Eastern Region of British Railways certainly took the nectar the long way round. The reasons of course are historical but it is nevertheless interesting to trace the path. Setting out from Burton it ran via Eggington Junction, Derby Friar Gate and Basford North from which point it climbed the steep spur to Bulwell Common South and then remained on the main line proceeding by way of Heath and Darnall where the Rotherham Branch was gained. By means of the junctions at Mexborough the Swinton & Knottingley Joint Line was reached for a direct run to York.

109. Bulwell Common, c.1952. An unidentified B1 class locomotive brings an up Manchester–Marylebone express across the blue brick viaduct alas recently demolished. This structure, so well illustrated by S.W.A. Newton in his splendid series of photographs showing the railway under construction, carried the line over the main road from Bulwell to Hucknall, the River Leen and the Midland Railway Mansfield Line which is out of sight below the third coach of the train. The tracks in the foreground connect Bulwell Common Station with the GN Leen Valley Line at Bestwood, the down line from Bulwell Common first burrowing below the GC mainline so as to form a junction as at Bagthorpe.

Photo: T.G. Hepburn

110. Bulwell Common, 16th September 1965. Although this photograph was taken in the declining years of the GC line, nevertheless the view from the south western corner of the layout shows that it remained intact to a remarkable degree. The station with island platform and public access from the road overbridge is in the distance and is flanked by sidings on both sides. It was here that the GC Company intended to build its locomotive shed at the turn of the century but found that the cost of land and the cost of a water supply particularly was too expensive. Taking into account the multiplicity of lines and sidings here it is difficult to see where the shed might have been located. The signal box basking in strong sunlight is Bulwell Common South Junction which has just despatched class 9F No. 92025 (8C) round the corner to Basford North with a train load of coal destined for Stanton Iron Works at Ilkeston. With the closing of the railway the land reverted to the ownership of the Nottingham City Council who have in turn sold off a vast majority of it to private developers who have virtually erased the whole of Bulwell Common from the map. If a landmark were required for those making a pilgrimage to the scene then it would be as well to know that the Golden Ball Public House is adjacent to the former entrance to Bulwell Common Station.   *Photo: D. Swale*

111. Bulwell Common, 18th August 1962. The Saturdays only Bradford to Poole train is in charge of a very clean LMS class 5 No. 44951 at the point where the up and down main lines diverge to accommodate the island platform of Bulwell Common Station. This is the view looking north from a point just west of the station showing Bulwell Common North Junction signal box in the foreground controlling the exit from the down loop to the down main, as well as the layout at the north end of the station which incorporates the junction put in to connect the GC Line with the GN Leen Valley Line at Moorbridge. The down GN Line drops behind the signal box before passing under the GC Main line in the distance. The up connection from Moorbridge comes in as a flat junction on the far right of the picture having passed through the cutting which appears above the third coach. Behind the photographer to the south of the road overbridge were located numerous sidings which also came under the control of the same signal box. In one of these sidings there used to stand a water crane invariably used by the Annesley Dido engine between its various tours of duty. The thoroughfare on the extreme left is called St. Alban's Road and along with the golf course on the extreme right represents the only feature illustrated here which still remains.

Whilst on the subject of Bulwell Common it should be mentioned that many of the people employed at Annesley sheds lived hereabouts, several miles away from their work with no public transport, hence the need for the Dido. However one interesting feature of the work concerned the question of relieving footplate crew working back to Annesley from Woodford. As is well known the Annesley–Woodford trains were originated by the LNER and ran on the basis that they left Annesley on time or were cancelled. All the more important then to get the men to work for if their train was cancelled they lost a day's pay. Sometimes however there would be a delay at the Woodford end and if the line was busy the return working with the empties might not get back to Annesley before the 8 hours were up. This meant one of two things. If the men continued through to Annesley with their train then a little bit of overtime would not come amiss, on the other-hand some drivers and firemen after an arduous trip preferred not to fly past their home and instead would sign off at Bulwell Common, which was perfectly acceptable, and then walk or cycle the short distance to where they lived. A spare crew would then be called upon to work the few remaining miles back to Annesley Yards.   *Photo: J. Cupit*

112. Bulwell Common, 18th August 1962. Class 01 No. 63817, an engine which for many years before the arrival of the 9Fs shared with its sisters the Annesley to Woodford Workings, now finds itself confined to less strenuous duties on a train of empties. The signal box is Bulwell Common South Junction viewed from the South Eastern corner of the layout there. The train proceeds along the up main towards Nottingham Victoria whilst the North to West curve connection with the original GN Derbyshire lines goes away to the left. *Photo: J. Cupit*

113. Bagthorpe Junction, 5th June 1954. One of the charming little J.5 engines, No. 65493, eases cautiously round the tight curves with wheel flanges squealing against the check rail on its emergence from the rat hole as it approaches Bagthorpe Junction with a stopping train from Pinxton to Nottingham. Even in the mid-1950's, when these engines were just as much at home in operating services of the type illustrated here as they were pottering about in Colwick yards on shunting duties, they seemed to belong to a different age altogether and were in striking contrast to the modern appearance of other engines on contemporary workings, for example, B.1s and L.1s both of which were no strangers to the Pinxton trains. *Photo: Author's collection*

114. Bagthorpe Junction, c.1962. Ninety yards proclaims the notice board as being the length of Basford Tunnel in this interesting view of 3 levels of track to the east of Basford North Station. A class 9F heads north up the grade on the GC mainline and will shortly be thundering through Bulwell Common with a clear run ahead having got the distant signal. The 9F is approaching the girder bridge which will carry it over the original GN Derbyshire lines extension from Colwick to Derby adjacent to which line a rake of non-corridor coaches is stored pending further use. Two junctions were effected between these lines, the West to North Junction climbing a gradient of 1 in 75 to Bulwell Common South Junction where a flat connection was made but the West to South connection was engineered in such a way so as not to affect Northbound traffic on the GC Line and hence a burrowing junction was required carrying the GN up line firstly under its own Colwick route and then under the GC mainline to make a connection at Bagthorpe Junction. This burrowing line was affectionately known as the Rat Hole. *Photo: R.W. Sheppard*

115. Bagthorpe Junction, 15th June 1963. The photographer has captured a panoramic view of Bagthorpe Junction, from the top of the sandstone cutting north of Perry Road Bridge, showing the Great Central Main Line heading away towards Annesley and the burrowing junction with the Great Northern's Line from Basford North. Trains for Pinxton or Derby and beyond took the line leading off to the left, whilst those travelling in the opposite direction having left Basford North burrowed under the Great Central Line before rising again on the track to the right of the signal box. The triangle of lines formed by Bagthorpe Junction, Basford North and Bulwell Common South Junction are being used in lieu of the Annesley turntable which was out of commission at this time, the purpose being to turn the three engines and return them to Annesley facing the right way to take up their next duties. One of the home sheds class 9F's is accompanied on this occasion by B16 No. 61434 from York, these two flanking an Austerity probably from Mexborough. *Photo: M.S. Castledine*

116. Bagthorpe Junction, c.1930. A local train from Grantham to Derby Friargate has a clear road signalled to its next stop at Basford North as it here approaches Bagthorpe Junction. The position of the shadows would seem to indicate a late afternoon working headed on this occasion by LNER class D2 No. 4329. These trains were usually made up of a set of articulated coaches with a brake at each end. On this occasion an additional separate brake vehicle is behind the tender but the remaining five form an articulated quintuple set. When the line was built attention was paid to detail so that even the line-side cabin carries finials to match those on the signal box. *Photo: T.G. Hepburn*

117. Bagthorpe Junction, n.d. In the years before the Second World War the LNER operated excursion trains for racegoers. This was hardly surprising because a number of famous racecourses were to be found within its territory including Newmarket, famous for sales of bloodstock as well as for racing, Wetherby, York and Thirsk all in the North of England and not the least Doncaster, home of the famous St. Leger Stakes run at the beginning of September in each year. Many special trains were run from the surrounding areas to such venues but the imaginative Publicity Department of the LNER developed the idea further not being afraid to organise longer distance trains to special events, the most famous of course being undoubtedly the Aintree Specials which always loaded well on Grand National Day. Nottingham's Race Course was out towards Colwick and several meetings were held each year enabling the Railway Company to organise first rate special trains to Racecourse Station adjacent to the action, a Station which did not appear in the timetable. These trains afforded luxury travel with restaurant car service no less. In this illustration the coaching stock for a return special to King's Cross is gingerly drawn out of a carriage siding by a large Atlantic No. 3286 joining the GCR main line at Bagthorpe Junction.   *Photo: T.G. Hepburn*

118. Bagthorpe Junction, n.d. Although designed and used as mixed traffic engines and much maligned in the railway press these GCR four cylinder 4-6-0s designed by Mr Robinson certainly looked impressive and provided a stirring sight when getting a train underway. No. 5073 thunders by with a down relief express tackling the adverse gradient on the first stretch of the climb from Nottingham towards Kirkby South Junction and belches out a sooty exhaust to the despair of adjacent housewives on a washday. Photographs do exist showing matters even worse; an illustration of one of the larger wheeled B.3s creating a deplorable black cloud comes to mind.
Photo: T.G. Hepburn

119. Bagthorpe Junction. The quality of the print is faultless but for once this is a scene which requires colour in order to do full justice. Eight minutes ago the Bournemouth to Newcastle express roared by, a substantial train whose engine would be showing visible signs of attacking the long climb to Kirkby, but lighter by three vehicles shown here detached at Nottingham. Assuming it is running to time the train left Victoria 5 minutes ago at 4.58pm, the coaches coming through from Bournemouth, but the train being shown in the timetable as an express passenger between Nottingham and Leeds. Although the rival LMS could offer reasonable connections to Bournemouth via the Somerset and Dorset Line from its Yorkshire stations, the LNER was quick to appreciate that its own service to Bournemouth only served the line between York and Sheffield thereby missing out on potential customers in the Leeds–Bradford area as well as in Doncaster. It was pointed out that a convenient route existed between Doncaster and Nottingham via the junction at Tuxford and Mansfield Central and if to this were added the Leeds to Doncaster portion then Wakefield and Mansfield could also be usefully served. In conjunction with the Southern Railway arrangements were made so that 2 trains each of 3 vehicles would be formed, each company providing a brake and 2 composite coaches. However, the arrangement was such that both trains conveyed a composite coach provided by each company in addition to one company's brake and rather than run a separate train south of Nottingham these vehicles would be attached to the through Newcastle to Bournemouth express in each direction. The train ran from at least 1927 until the outbreak of the Second World War. In this splendid view the pristine Atlantic No. 4453 showing off its smart apple green livery heads first of all 2 teak coaches furnished with headboards as befits a train of its class, trailed by a composite coach in Southern Railway green thus enhancing the colourful spectacle. The signalman at Bagthorpe Junction box located on the east side of the line and about to be passed by the train has very swiftly returned his signal to danger. Although not from his own camera, Jack Cupit, some of whose work appears in this book , recounts with fond memories his days at Newgate Lane School, Mansfield, fortunately placed adjacent to the railway line, remembering that many were the occasions when his mind was distracted from lessons in the late morning as the up train was due to pass by.

Photo: T.G Hepburn

120. New Basford, 13th August 1956. The ridge of high ground through which Sherwood Rise Tunnel had to be driven stands out well in the background beyond the carriage sidings and the station at New Basford. Having passed both of these features class J11/3 No. 64354 heads north with a short mixed train. The carriage sidings at Basford held the responsibility to provide the coaching stock for all local services on the ex-LNER Lines in the Nottingham area together with some main line stock which at weekends would be put to good use on excursion traffic.

Photo: Author's collection

121. New Basford, 25th July 1964. Jubilee No. 45562 *Alberta* must surely have been the most photographed engine in its class, when it enjoyed an Indian summer of working from Holbeck shed in Leeds and could often be seen on the photogenic Pennine route between Skipton and Carlisle. However a year or two before those events it appeared quite regularly at Nottingham Victoria, working the Saturdays only summer train from Bradford to Poole. The layover at Nottingham allowed time to get the fire in good order for the return trip starting with the 10 miles or so against the collar to Kirkby South Junction. Smoke clings to the mouth of Sherwood Rise Tunnel as the locomotive heads the northbound working where the up and down lines separate from each other in typical GC fashion at New Basford. To judge by the exhaust the engine seems to be well into its stride and obviously there was still some pride in appearance, in these days when the all-conquering diesel was in the ascendancy. *Photo: M.S. Castledine*

122. New Basford, 15th August 1964. Great Western motive power was not entirely unknown in Nottingham and several photographs exist of Hall Class locomotives at or near to Nottingham Victoria. Occasionally one would arrive on Annesley shed on a Saturday in circumstances where its return working was not until the Monday, which on one memorable occasion resulted in the visiting Hall engine being turned out to work a Sunday ballast train near to Mansfield Central. However, perhaps the most unusual working of all was on the 15th August 1964, when, instead of the usual LMS Jubilee from Farnley Junction shed, Leeds, the GWR engine worked beyond Nottingham on the 8.55am Saturday train from Bournemouth West to Leeds. The Jubilee was not available to take up the normal return working from Nottingham in the early afternoon and for some reason the station pilot/standby engine could not be called upon to substitute. The train was running fairly well to time at Nottingham so the Annesley crew were not at all perturbed when called upon to work No. 6858 *Woolston Grange* on to Sheffield. The schedule to Sheffield Victoria was not very demanding and the train drew to a halt there on time but not without the cylinder cover fouling the concrete platform edging on arrival. The damage was only slight and did not incapacitate the locomotive, but it was unexpected for a GWR Hall had worked regularly between Marylebone and Sheffield in the 1948 locomotive exchanges. However, noticing the slight mishap and observing the unfamiliar outlines of the steed, the relief driver from Huddersfield steadfastly refused to have anything to do with taking the train forward with this engine, no doubt fearing further incidents along the way. Again, as luck would have it, Sheffield could offer no relief engine, and a decision was made to continue as far as Huddersfield with the Grange being driven by a Locomotive Inspector who, according to contemporary reports, was dressed in a blue pinstripe suit, assisted by the Huddersfield fireman. Proceeding via Penistone the foray was cut short at Huddersfield where *Woolston Grange* came off the train and went on shed where it aroused a good deal of curiosity over the succeeding few days whilst the North Eastern Region people worked out the conundrum of getting it back home without further accident. One of the authors who was a passenger in the train north of Nottingham was told that the engine was sent via Stockport to Crewe and handed over there to people more accustomed to copper capped chimneys and the like. *Photo: M.S. Castledine*

123. New Basford, 3rd September 1949. Perhaps the best known of all the cross country trains was the Bournemouth. Two sets of coaches were used provided respectively by the Southern and the North Eastern Regions of the newly formed British Railways. This continued an arrangement which had been made in the enterprising years before the 1923 grouping when Sir Sam Fay held the post of general manager on the GCR. The train always ran between Bournemouth and York but at certain times it was extended beyond York to Newcastle. The operation of the train at the time of this photograph involved the use of at least 4 locomotives, a typical northbound run setting off behind a King Arthur class yielding to a GWR Hall at Oxford. Between Leicester and Sheffield a Low Moor engine worked by a Sheffield crew was involved with the final leg to York being often worked by one of that sheds B16s. Looking very smart indeed No. 45208 tackles the northbound climb from Nottingham with the Southern Region's rolling stock.
Photo: J.F. Henton

124. Carrington, c.1956. Limited space between Mansfield Road and Sherwood Rise tunnels provided just enough room to squeeze in the station at Carrington. For once this London extension station was not the island platform variety but a cursory glance at the photograph offers its own explanation. The signal box was provided here to break up the block section between Victoria North and New Basford and thereby increased the line capacity in the middle of the bottle neck. In fact the signal box was located almost exactly midway between those adjacent the distance in each direction being approximately 1250 yards and in 1939 it was open continuously between the early hours of Monday morning and 4.00am the following Sunday. Carrington Station became an early casualty to competition from road transport with the LNER taking the decision to close it in 1929. No more did a few trains in each direction pause briefly here on their suburban journeys and one might speculate that the operating authorities were greatly relieved when passengers were no longer welcomed here. Class A.5 No. 69822 was merely passing through on its approach to Nottingham Victoria. Most of the houses in the picture are now used either for hotels, nursing homes or accountants' offices, but once more this corner of the city is changing with a provision of further office accommodation on the very site of the station. Public access at road level high above the north portal of Mansfield Road tunnel has for many years past enjoyed its present use as a retail shop.
Photo: J.R. Bonsor

125. Victoria. Drivers eye view of the northern approach to Victoria Station taken from just inside Mansfield Road tunnel and showing the crossover line in the tunnel mouth. In earlier years the picture would have been enhanced by a gantry spanning the approach tracks carrying an array of GCR pattern semaphores.
Photo: Author's collection

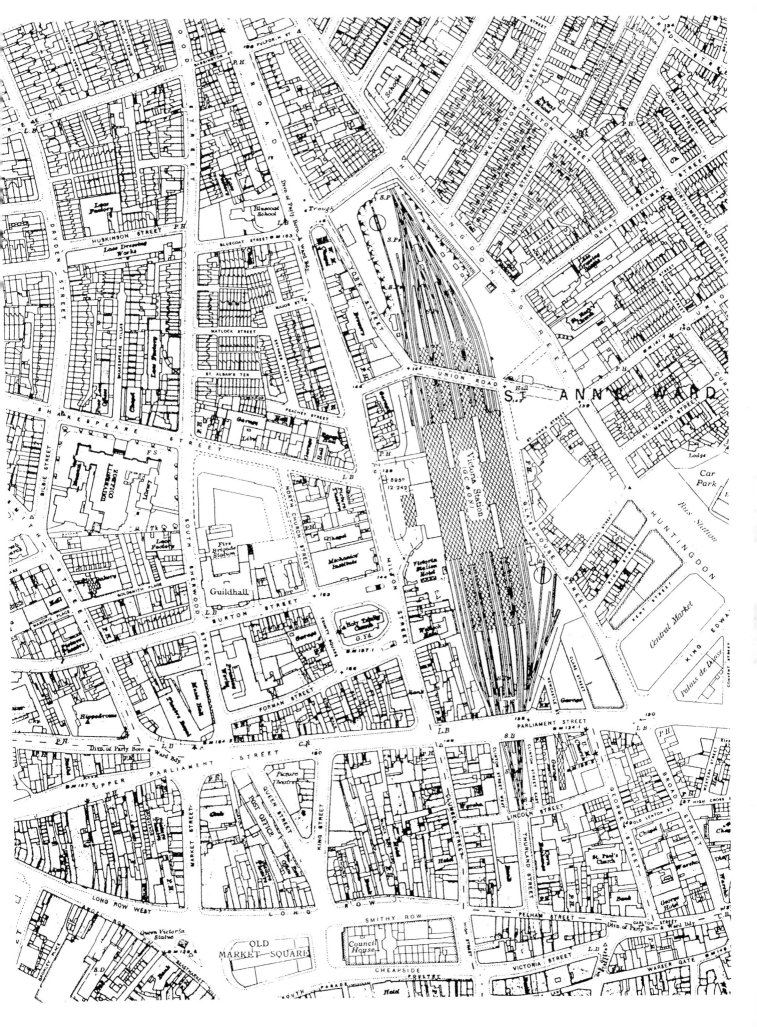

26. Victoria. A 9F steals quietly along the up main and passes an L1 simmering gently in the middle road. The engines are not important for it s the atmosphere in this photograph which is all pervading. It was large yet ever remote, busy but not hurried, tall and cathedral like but in no way unfriendly. In the mid 1950s "the Vic" was a comfortable place to be and ve all thought it would last for ever.

NOTTINGHAM VICTORIA

To usurp a phrase from Hamilton Ellis "Victoria was a magnificent station". It was of course built to serve the quite different needs of two railway companies and its construction and operation was done under the auspices of a joint committee whose directors were appointed by the two owning companies. The Manchester, Sheffield and Lincolnshire Railway as it then was had penetrated as far south as Annesley in 1892 at which point an end on junction was made with the Leen Valley Line of the Great Northern Railway, but in the following year parliament had authorised the construction of this country's last main line from Annesley to Quainton Road which was to form the major part of the London extension. The company name was changed to Great Central Railway in 1897 in anticipation of the opening of the line which would not be long delayed. No attempt was made to develop feeder lines because its partner the Great Northern Railway was already well enough established in the Nottingham area and would be linked to the new route at Bulwell and also to the south of the new station at Weekday Cross.

To accommodate the Great Central's Expresses two through platforms would suffice but in the provision of extensive sidings at Annesley and a large marshalling yard at Woodford in Northamptonshire it is clear that a substantial volume of goods and mineral traffic was likely to be carried south, all of which would require to pass through the station.

The need of the GNR was rather different in that London Road was inconveniently placed for the city centre and all services operated by that company to points north and west of Nottingham were forced to commence with an inconvenient detour over the stiffly graded suburban railway or on a longer but busier route via Gedling. There was also the operating inconvenience because London Road was a terminus. The new section of line through London Road high level to Weekday Cross was an expensive project carried for the most part on bridges or viaducts towards the Broad Marsh area of the city where several buildings had to be cleared away, but by joining in the new venture and by the provision of the new connections already referred to the Great Northern not only rid itself of all these problems but was now able to convey passengers to and from the heart of the city and many local passenger services entered the new station at one end and left it at the other on a continuous circuit.

The GCR awarded the contract for the section of the new line through Nottingham to Messrs Logan & Hemmingway but the execution of station works as normal was put out to separate competitive tender and the Joint Committee entrusted the contract to Mr Henry Lovatt of Wolverhampton who was to work under the direction of Edward Parry, an eminent member of the Institute of Civil Engineers, who, together with three assistants, was responsible for the design and architectural detail of the station. Some of Nottingham's worst slums had to be cleared away before any work could be done at all and this involved lengthy negotiations for the acquisition of land, the demolition of about 1300 dwellings, some 24 licensed premises and the Nottingham Union Work House built in 1840 which stood at the corner of York Street and Woodborough Road. As a result some streets disappeared for good including Charlotte Street, Balloon Court, Milk Square, Salmon Yard and Bear Court. It was a term of the authorising legislation that sufficient dwellings should be provided to re-house the people so displaced and this resulted in further development of the Meadows area close by Arkwright Street Station and also the building of the houses on Watkin Street near to Woodborough Road. This street of course bore the name of the chairman of the Manchester, Sheffield and Lincolnshire Railway, Sir Edward Watkin, who visualised the new line as part of a through rail route between Manchester and Paris, Channel Tunnel and all! Excavations were deeper at the Woodborough Road end of the area set aside for the new station and the rock much harder which explains why no high masonry walls were provided near the mouth of Mansfield Road Tunnel such as were necessary along part of the eastern perimeter. Over 500,000 cubic yards of predominantly sandstone was excavated and had to be carted away for only when this stage had been reached was it possible for Mr Lovatt to make satisfactory progress.

The main frontage of the station was to Mansfield Road, almost opposite the end of Shakespeare Street. Sufficient space was allowed between the highway and the frontage of the main buildings to allow for Hackney carriages and the like to be accommodated in a front court yard most of which was covered by a functional canopy which unfortunately hid part of the attractive station façade. Materials used were Darley Dale stone and best quality faced bricks from the Nottingham Patent Brick Company with which, of course, Edward Parry was strongly associated. The renaissance style of architecture was adopted but with a strong Jacobean flavour, its three storey height being exceeded quite deliberately by the

continued over

impressive square profile clock tower executed in matching brick with cupola rising to more than 100 feet and finished off with a weather vane exposed to the wind from all quarters. At the north end of the frontage access to the parcels office and the yard was through a pair of wrought iron gates which had the initials of the two owning companies cut out of the metal work. By means of two metalled ramps also in this vicinity access was given to a carriage and horse dock which was met by similar facilities on the eastern side of the station with access from Parliament Street. Once inside the buildings at road level, the spacious booking hall was encountered with seven ticket issuing positions, one for excursion traffic and the other six shared equally between GN and GC Companies. Over 100 foot long and some 66 feet wide it was panelled in best quality pine to a height of about 11 feet whilst some 20 feet or so above the hard wearing oak block floor, a delicate balcony ran across part of the length to happily punctuate the overall height of 35 feet and from this balcony it was possible to pass from one office to another. When the adjacent hotel was opened in September 1901 a covered passage led directly to it from the booking hall. Having purchased a ticket the traveller made his way towards the platforms but could if he wished send his luggage ahead by using one of the two hydraulic lifts which connected with the subway system, a little known feature of this great station. This subway was also used for mails and parcels and was truly located in the bowels of the station below rail level connecting the main station buildings with the two island platforms approximately along the route of the old Charlotte Street. It was of generous proportions being 14 feet wide and almost as high with walls of glazed brick. By this means the movement of parcels and luggage

particularly from one part of the station to the other would not impede passengers anxious to be on their way.

From the booking hall the platforms were approached by means of a wide steel footbridge which spanned the running lines at right angles and projected all the way to the second entrance of the station on Glasshouse Street which was hardly ever used, its stout doors being firmly bolted as far back as memory goes. Originally Victoria was an open station with tickets being checked at Arkwright Street or Carrington, this arrangement did not suit the GNR and it is thought that the ticket barrier which everyone remembers was brought into use in the station's infancy. The long standing public right of way between Mansfield Road and Huntingdon Street was to be found in an enclosed bridge running parallel and to the north of the one just described, and it is to the credit of the contractors that this footpath was kept available for use during the time the station was being built. The two bridges were connected on the west side of the station by a pedestrian gangway supported by girders but again this was hardly ever used, the iron gate adjacent to the public footway being bolted except at very busy times for example Goose Fair.

Returning to the main passenger footbridge this was connected by stairways on either side leading down to the two main island platforms, each paved from end to end, a distance of 1270 feet, according to a contemporary report with "granolithic flags". The maximum width of the platform was 68 feet, the more westerly one being flanked by through platform numbers 1 and 4 serving northbound trains, the other one being enclosed by number 7 and 10 platforms dealing with the up direction. Indented into each end of the island platform were 2 bays giving a total of 8 additional platforms

127. Victoria, c.1954. Engines of ex. Great Eastern design were not common visitors, but here an admittedly rebuilt member of the class which was the pride of the Sweedie, as the GER was called by many railwaymen, B12 No. 61554 has been sent out by Grantham shed on one of its turns along the Nottingham line. This photograph also shows to advantage the attractive buildings following their post-war cleaning some fifty years of grime being removed from the glazed bricks. The low ellipse as used for the windows was an architectural feature in vogue at the end of last century, often to be seen on other railway buildings, for example on most of the stations between Chesterfield and Lincoln on the erstwhile Lancashire Derbyshire & East Coast Railway.   *Photo: F. Ashley*

which could be used for arrival and departure of stopping trains. Within these bays crossovers were provided when the station was built but due to the signalling arrangements in the middle of the station adjacent to the passenger footbridge each through platform could accommodate 2 shorter trains at any one time, and by means of further crossovers the up or down passenger loop could be used to enable one train to depart in advance of the one standing directly ahead of it. All this mean that the bays were underused and as time went by those at the south end of platform 1 and the north end of platform 10 were largely unused for departures.

The middle portion of the platform for a distance of 420 feet between the north and south bays was covered by an enormous glazed roof supported by robust steel pillars and divided across the width of the station area into 3 impressive spans the two outer being some 63 feet and the central span between the two island platforms about 21 feet more than this, high enough above platform level at about 40 feet to create a feeling of airiness and space which belied the fact that the station was effectively built in a hole. At either end of this magnificent roof glass screens existed which were very soon coated in soot from the engine exhausts. Once beyond the glazed screens travellers were still protected from rain by awnings which extended over all the bay platforms for a distance of 224 feet.

Four very similar blocks of buildings existed, two on each island in each case one either side of the central footbridge giving an appearance of symmetry. In fact the two more northerly blocks are the closest to being identical in that they each comprised at the lower level four waiting rooms and a set of lavatories but on the up side the general waiting room was reduced in size to accommodate the east signal cabin. All upper floors found use as offices of one kind or another and were out of bounds to the travelling public. Below the offices to the south of the passenger footbridge the rooms were put to different uses according to whether one was on the up or down island. Taking the down side buildings first these housed the bay windowed west signal cabin which was adjacent to the station master office, itself most conveniently located close to everything of importance. Also in this block at least into the LNER period could be found adjacent refreshment rooms segregated for use by first and third class passengers respectively. A lavatory block and store room corresponding with similar facilities on the up side completed the picture. On platform 7 one found a refreshment room presumably for use by all classes, together with separate accommodation for diners, and yet another catering facility delightfully called a Ladies Tea Room. Nottingham girls are some of the prettiest in England, so it is said, and we would not wish to take issue with that but wonder if that is the reason why the late Victorian railway builders went to such lengths to accommodate the ladies. If a man were boldly to venture into one of the rooms set aside for the fair sex he would in all probability transgress the railway byelaws. Adjacent to the Ladies Tea Room was the Telegraph Office, a most important centre of information and activity, later transferred to the down side. All rooms and offices were lit by electricity from the outset and there was even a little building where foot warmers were stored and prepared. Taken as a whole and viewed in the nature of life as it existed at the turn of the century every passenger comfort was provided for those waiting to travel, even if the coaches which they boarded were not up to Midland Railway standards.

Train movements at Nottingham Victoria were controlled by 4 cabins of which the east and west platform boxes with 27 and 18 levers respectively have already been mentioned. Nottingham Victoria South occupied a gloomy position close to Parliament Street Road Bridge which denied a good deal of natural light to the staff who were obliged to offer on some 300 trains per day using 85 levers in the process.

Much more fortunate were their colleagues in the uniquely shaped north signal cabin, so constructed to accommodate the tighter bottleneck adjacent to Mansfield Road Tunnel but at least they were out in the open and had a clearer view of the part of the layout controlled by their 87 levers. Its position also resulted in its frequent appearance on photographs concerned with the station.

Because the station was jointly owned this fact was reflected in the staffing of the two main cabins which, in the days prior to 1923 were operated in such a way that if a Great Central man was on duty in the north box there would be a Great Northern signalman operating Victoria south. In those days two Great Northern and one Great Central man covered the North signal box, whilst at the South end the ratio was the opposite way around. The signalling apparatus however was in true Great Central style and it was always a delight to go down to the station even into the 1960's to see the lower quadrant semaphore arms, two of which at least in the centre of the up and down main platforms survived to the bitter end. At one time

continued over

128. Victoria, 20 August 1967. The frontage of the station as seen from Shakespeare Street with a City Transport bus passing along Mansfield Road. When the station was removed from the face of the earth to make way for the Victoria Shopping Centre and flats (the latter having recently been described as one of the worst examples of modern building) the rectangular clock tower was spared to survive, not as a proud beacon shown here, but sadly as an incongruous pile overlooked and indeed overwhelmed by the monstrosity of the 1970s. At one stage of its post railway career it suffered the ignominy of being part of 'The Reject Shop', and there are those who say it would have been kinder to have removed it with the rest of the station.

129. Victoria, 2nd November 1965. Barrows carrying a few mailbags on either side of the door to the goods lift provide the only sign of life in this nocturnal view of the up main platform. An eerie stillness can be sensed in this floodlit cathedral of wrought iron with the signal arm lowered as if for the passage of a ghost train.

there was a splendid gantry controlling trains coming in through Mansfield Road Tunnel with a galaxy of signal arms reminiscent of the Northeastern Railway manner of doing things and this spanned the lines between the north cabin and the tunnel mouth.

The story is well known as to how the station came to aquire its name. The Great Central not surprisingly wished to call it Nottingham Central keeping not only with its newly acquired title (it had been the MS&L Railway till 1897) but because the station was central to the city as well. The Great Northern was not impressed and, having spent a great deal of capital on the project thought that a more striking name should be used, the Town Clerk intervened with the acceptable suggestion that because the opening of the station took place on the Queen's birthday and because the station was a fitting monument to late Victorian enterprise it deserved to be called Nottingham Victoria. Hitherto it was called Nottingham Joint Station as evidenced by a report in the Nottingham Daily Guardian on the day of opening. A medallion issued by Jessop and Son of Nottingham commemorated the opening of the station but on the face of this it was referred to as "Central". Open for business at last, the Nottingham Joint Station Committee had indeed done the city proud.

May 24th 1900, this was the day the GNR had been waiting for. With immediate effect it transferred all its passenger business in the Nottingham area from London Road (by now known as London Road Low Level) into the new Joint Station, in anticipation whereof Messrs. Waterlow & Sons Ltd of London printed for the Company a thirteen page Timetable detailing the new arrangements for its trains in the "Nottinghamshire, Derbyshire & Leicestershire Districts". It was at pains to point out that the LNWR trains between Nottingham and Northampton would still use "London Road, Low Level, Station", a situation which continued until 1944.

The GNR was involved in the operation of four expresses in each direction between Nottingham and London Kings Cross in liaison with the GCR. In the up direction the through train from Sheffield left Nottingham at 10.15am and was due in the metropolis at 1.05pm. The other three trains

originated at Manchester and were booked to leave Nottingham Joint Station at 12.14pm, 4.22pm and 7.18pm, the first and last of these being described as Luncheon Car Express and Dining Car Express respectively. Apart from these the GNR passenger workings were of a local nature, serving all its various lines, by that time well established. Through trains to Stafford or Burton-on-Trent went by way of Derby Friargate, one of the fastest services being the 4.15pm through train from Grantham advertised as connecting with the 2pm ex-Kings Cross, and this left Nottingham at 5.10pm on a 29 minute schedule to Derby calling only at Ilkeston. By comparison with the service from Nottingham Midland the timing to Derby was respectable but the MR had the better connections at the end of the journey for people needing to travel further. To Ilkeston of course the GNR had much the quicker route; however, in fairness, it should be pointed out that the MR establishment there was at the end of a short branch line from the Erewash Valley. A comparison of the rival services between Nottingham and Newark shows the boot to be on the other foot, for whilst the MR had the edge in time, it was the GNR which offered better connections at its Northgate Station. The Suburban line was catered for as well as the branch to Pinxton and the line up the Leen Valley to Newstead, which service had been extended to Skegby on the company's final development in the East Midlands. Soon it would reach Shirebrook (later known as Shirebrook South) and eventually the final development took the form of through trains between Nottingham and Chesterfield (Market Place) by way of Langwith Junction (later Shirebrook North) worked on occasions by Steam Railcars. Parcels supplemented GNR passenger trade but goods and mineral trains were kept well clear remaining on the "Back Line" via Gedling. The GCR for its part did not concern itself with what would now be termed commuter traffic, indeed it built no branch lines anywhere near to Nottingham, nor would it have been necessary to do this as they were already provided by its partner in the new enterprise. It is true to say that the GCR agreed to work the Mansfield Railway, opened throughout in 1917, presumably on the basis that it connected with its own

130. Victoria, 18th September 1964. The booking hall with its fixtures and fittings which were to be found at any main line station, including the brightly lit W.H. Smith kiosk, railway trolleys and automatic vending machines, typical of the era. The two litter bins, however, look somewhat out of place. Behind the gallery are located the rooms used as offices by the local railway top brass.

Photo: D. Thompson

lines at both ends, having already absorbed the independent Lancashire, Derbyshire & East Coast Railway, known as the "Dukeries Route", with effect from the beginning of 1907. A local service from the city to Sutton-in-Ashfield and Mansfield was put on providing those growing towns with a shorter journey time than the MR was able to achieve. Even so, wider horizons were considered resulting in Mansfield being treated to its first and only through Breakfast Car express to London Marylebone. It appears that the Great Central's drive southwards was fuelled by three primary objectives. Firstly, and most importantly, it was to muscle in on the very substantial movement of coal especially to the London area and in so doing take the opportunity to develop ancillary goods services for the carriage of other merchandise and raw materials. Secondly it fulfilled its ambition to become a trunk route to the capital, which thus gained additional services to Manchester, Sheffield and other northern towns as well as Nottingham. Finally the short but vital link to the GWR at Banbury from Culworth Junction opened up wide possibilities for the operation of through trains or carriages from the north of England to places as far apart as South Wales and the Hampshire coast. This opportunity was seized upon without delay by the Company's General Manager, Sam Fay, later knighted, who negotiated agreements between his own masters and principally the North Eastern and Great Western Railways to establish the renowned cross country services, which may now be recalled.

These splendid trains were held in high regard by those who travelled on them, many of whom would be undertaking journeys between two intermediate points. For example it would be wrong to suppose that everyone entraining at York wanted to get to Bournemouth or vice versa. This train offered a new and convenient means of getting from York to Nottingham; by the same token University students might be resident in Leicester, but graduating at Oxford. No longer was it necessary to change trains en route. The LNER had no qualms about perpetuating the services initiated prior to 1923, and there is no reason to suppose that they would have discontinued them had it not been for the intervention of the second

world war. It is proposed to look at them as existing in May 1939 by reference to Bradshaw's Railway Guide.

A Restaurant Car express left Newcastle at quarter past eight in the morning and reached GCR territory by way of York and Swinton & Knottingley Joint line, being due to appear at platform 7 at 12.28pm. A though coach from Hull which had come by way of Pontefract was collected on the way and at Nottingham three vehicles from Leeds by way of Doncaster and the Mansfield Railway were added to the train making its strength ten corridor coaches. A stop of only six minutes was allowed before the train was on its way to Bournemouth going via Oxford and Southampton. Next in sequence came the "Ports to Ports" express which changed engines at Victoria before departing at 1.55pm as it had done for many years. The title was unofficial. Pursuant to a complicated working agreement between the GCR and its North Eastern and GWR partners a new service between Newcastle on Tyne and Cardiff was inaugurated in 1906. The formation of this Restaurant Car express for which two sets of brand new rolling stock were built, was five bogie coaches, but quite often it appeared with one or two extra vehicles at the head of the basic formation. A through coach from Hull to Swansea is shown in the timetable for May 1939 as being included in the train which, after leaving Banbury, took the Cotswold line to Cheltenham before proceeding after Gloucester, by way of Cardiff and Barry on its tortuous ramble.

Late afternoon saw the arrival of a through Restaurant Car express from Newcastle to Oxford, but this included coaches starting out from Glasgow reaching Newcastle by way of Edinburgh and continued beyond Oxford and Basingstoke on Mondays, Wednesdays and Fridays to Southampton Docks to connect with cross channel steamers. Departure from Nottingham was at 5.21pm. Just over three hours later at 8.33pm another cross country train drifted in through Mansfield Road tunnel, which included in its formation the through coach from Aberdeen to Penzance, the longest possible rail journey then available in Great Britain

continued over

131. Victoria, c.1962. Better and busier days are a thing of the past and the impression portrayed is of a station much underused. The London Midland Region of BR thought enough of the place to rid it of Eastern Region colours, and on acquisition in 1958, resolved to bedeck the station with its own regional colour, hence the maroon enamel nameboard. Note the five-legged platform seat which was perhaps the only one of its kind. This pattern, with six legs of course, was originally manufactured by Messrs Andrew Handyside and adopted as standard by both the Great Central and Midland Railway companies.   *Photo: G.H. Platt*

without having to change, although how many people withstood the whole journey is open to debate. A vital facility was the restaurant car put on between Glasgow and York, which then continued as far as Swindon. The train was allowed five minutes to complete station business at Nottingham.

Last one of these remarkable trains was decidedly a creature of the night leaving York at 10.13pm and destined for Bristol via Oxford and Swindon. Several vehicles were reserved for the volume of parcels carried, hence lengthy station stopovers so progress was relatively slow. Some 18 minutes were spent occupying platform 7, which this train vacated well after midnight, at six minutes to one. Each of the trains described had a northbound counterpart, but the essential feature to remember is that they operated every weekday throughout the year, and were not merely summer or weekend services. On Sundays matters were radically altered and only the long established Sheffield to Swansea train appeared, the LNER engine from Sheffield (Neepsend) depot working through to Swindon. Before the war this caused the rather unfamiliar outline of either a B17 Footballer or a GN Large Atlantic to turn a few heads in Swindon of a Sunday afternoon! In the BR era a Darnall B1 worked this train to Swindon, and, due to civil engineering works would sometimes be delayed or diverted away from the accepted route. Certainly there have been times when, prior to reaching Nottingham, this train has taken the difficult diversionary line through Spinkhill and Pleasley.

"Daffy down dilly has come up to Town,
in a brown petticoat and a green gown".

This somewhat derogatory comment referred to the opening of Marylebone station in 1899, the colours quoted being relevant to the smart livery worn by contemporary GCR engines. Comfortable, smartly-timed lightweight expresses were the order of the day for many years operating between Marylebone and either Sheffield or Manchester. Bradford via Huddersfield got a through train, and in time, so did Mansfield, whilst Halifax benefitted by acquiring a through coach. For very many years these workings were the preserve of the graceful Atlantic type locomotive designed by Mr. Robinson, many of which were based at Leicester where most trains changed engines. In this manner Leicester shed and its crews developed a love for and understanding of the Jersey Lilies by which name the class came to be known, which was second to none. However, with noticeably heavier loadings in the 1930s the Class B17s bearing names of football teams were allocated in quantity to the London Extension causing Leicester shed with some reluctance to find other less exacting work for their beloved Atlantics.

Before the outbreak of war a few Gresley Pacifics and V2s appeared and these took over the workings of most London expresses. The May 1939 Bradshaw gives departures from Marylebone as follows:–

2.32am newspaper train which called at Arkwright Street to offload the dailys.

8.45am express to Manchester.

10.00am express to Sheffield and Bradford.

12.15pm to Manchester.

3.20pm to Manchester dubbed by Railwaymen "Sam Fay Special".

4.55pm to Manchester, unofficially referred to as "Promptitude".

6.20pm to Sheffield and Bradford.

In the opposite direction trains left Manchester for London at 8.20am, 2.20pm and 3.50pm. There was a 10.00am departure from Bradford and a 7.30am from Sheffield both running through to Marylebone, the latter reaching the capital at 10.40am, some eight minutes ahead of the 7.36am from Nottingham which originated at Mansfield at 6.56am, and which train it had trailed for most of the way.

Excursion trains were always a feature of travel from Victoria Station. Just about every weekend in the summer season several were put on to the Lincolnshire seaside resorts, some commencing at Victoria, whilst others would begin their journeys at Pinxton, Pleasley, Ilkeston or some outlying town, calling at several points in the Nottingham area to pick up families and their excited children. Such trains were both popular and cheap offering a good day out in the years when most of us did not have a motor car. Particular interests were not overlooked and race specials to Uttoxeter, York and Market Rasen come readily to mind. A football match in the city

132. Victoria, c.1960's. GCR pattern lower quadrant signals control train movements along the western perimeter of the station, remarkably enough with all finials intact. A similar gantry on the up lines received upper quadrant arms a some stage. Despite the number of signal arms on display in this view, the main line signals in the middle of the main up and down lines with their smaller calling on arms may be better remembered.
Photo: G.H. Platt

would always generate a few extra trains, some to carry the local supporters from the outlying villages, others to bring the away team fans from more distant parts, which had the benefit of producing unusual engine workings. Occasionally the local extras would call at London Road (High Level) or Arkwright Street, both of which were closer to the grounds, especially Meadow Lane, the home of Notts County, than was Victoria. However, fans who chose to get out at Nottingham Victoria would invariably make their way to the south end of platform 7 and leave by the station's third exit, direct onto Parliament Street, where buses would be waiting to take them on with their rattles and scarves as far as Trent Bridge, which was convenient for both grounds.

The exit to Parliament Street appears in the illustrations within this book (Plate 134) and took the form of a covered staircase from the south end of platforms 4 and 7 leading up to a connecting footbridge adjacent to the road. There was no ticket office here, nor for that matter any other facility, but season ticket holders or workers with return tickets made much use of it because it was more conveniently located for offices, shops and markets than was the main entrance fronting Mansfield Road. Its wooden doors were closed for the last time on 18 April 1959, and soon afterwards a new building appeared at the same spot, visible in Plate 136.

The Marylebone line was the most convenient for events at Wembley Stadium, so it is not surprising to find that in the post grouping and nationalisation periods excursions to F.A. Cup Finals and International Football matches frequently used the GC route. Perhaps it was this proximity to Wembley which persuaded the LNER to give the B17s allocated new to the line the names of football clubs? Another event which added further variety to the scene was the exchange of locomotives organised in 1948 by the then new British Railways whereby locomotives from various regions were put to work over lines where they did not normally appear, for the purposes of comparison. Manchester to Marylebone was one such route selected for testing, and this brought a Southern Pacific, a GWR Hall and an LMS Black Five in the mixed traffic category to compete with the indigenous B1.

In the post war period two named trains operated through Victoria Station every weekday, and it is perhaps these as opposed to any others for which the line will be best remembered by the majority of people reading this book. The 7.30am Sheffield to Marylebone express of pre-war years reappeared in the winter 1947 timetable as a 7.40am departure titled most

appropriately *The Master Cutler*. Several Gresley Pacifics now of Class A3 were stationed at Leicester and took their turn in the working of this prestigious train. No. 60104 *Solario*, 60111 *Enterprise* and 60059 *Tracery* were among the favourites. The return working left London at 6.15pm and having enjoyed dinner on the train Sheffield was reached at about ten o'clock, the actual time varying a few minutes over the years. The Eastern Region decided to put on a faster diesel hauled service from Sheffield to London Kings Cross via Retford in 1958, an all Pullman service to which the title of *Master Cutler* was transferred. The new venture was reminiscent of the short lived Sheffield Pullman of 1924, an unsuccessful attempt by the LNER to provide an exclusive service from Sheffield to Kings Cross, picking up at Nottingham en route. It seems strange to relate that the name *Master Cutler* continues to find favour even to this day, moreover still applied to the morning executive inter city train from Sheffield to St. Pancras and the early evening return. You have to travel first class today in order to partake of breakfast; this is not an improvement on circumstances in the 1950s!

The only other officially named train to run on the GC line was the *South Yorkshireman*. The name was bestowed by BR, and being first used in 1948, it was applied to the train which was the direct successor to the pre-war 10.00am Bradford to Marylebone, which still remained faithful to the ten o'clock departure time. It brought a Low Moor engine as far as Sheffield via Huddersfield and Penistone, which there yielded the train to a Darnall B1, always very clean as it emerged into the daylight from Mansfield Road tunnel just before half past twelve. Normally loaded to ten bogies the return working set off from Marylebone at 4.50pm being tightly timed to reach Sheffield in 3 hours and 6 minutes. As the years went by the schedule was eased, and eventually in the run down of the GC line the train was taken off and the name was lost for ever.

It is no easy task to catalogue the various types of motive power passing through Victoria Station, for to do this would be to produce an interminably long list. We are not going to attempt this, but would ask the reader to study the illustrations which represent some of the typical locomotive types found on the LNER lines around Nottingham. It is clearly not possible to include every type which worked through the station on a regular basis and there are bound to be favourites which are absent from this book. One or two surprises would be found on any such list as might

continued over

133. Nottingham Victoria, 1950. The grandeur of "Vic" was evident in nearly all aspects of the station as this view shows of the panelled façade of the Booking Hall.

be prepared so perhaps by way of example the occasion when three Southern Pacifics turned up on the same day should be recounted. The inability of Nottingham Forest Football Club to resolve a cup tie with Southampton at the first attempt explains why three special trains were arranged to bring away supporters to the replay in Nottingham, on Saturday 30th March 1963. These specials all comprising green liveried Southern Region stock had arrived by half past one with the engines being sent forward to Annesley to be serviced. Punctually at 5.40pm No. 43059 set off for Grantham with the only remaining steam working on that line then through the murk and drizzle the strange outline of an unrebuilt Bulleid Pacific at the head of thirteen coaches followed it into platform 7. No. 34054 *Lord Beaverbrook* took on water ready for the non stop run to Banbury. Whilst this was going on rebuilt engine No. 34042 *Dorchester* brought the second train into number 10 platform comprising twelve vehicles to form the 6.15pm departure. Two strangers in the camp side by side . . . what a spectacle! Unfortunately neither was clean, both were shrouded in steam, and the attendant gloom made photography impossible. Attention was then drawn to a Black Five from Crewe North shed busying itself with the circus train, shunting the special wagons emblazoned with the name Bertram Mills Circus into position by the east side loading dock. Some camels were proving to be stubborn, refusing to venture forth onto the streets of Nottingham, doubtless on account of the adverse weather. The last of the trio, ten coaches hauled by Unrebuilt Pacific No. 34102 *Lapford* occupied platform 10 for 25 minutes making a punctual exit at 6.45pm, and although it was cleaner than its sisters, by now the light had gone. This was the character of Nottingham Vic . . . full of surprises.

The outermost though lines were designated goods loops. The GC section goods and mineral trains were obliged to come this way and over the years many millions of tons of coal flowed south hauled by six and eight coupled engines of GC design. Wagons laden with coal mined at the pits of Nottinghamshire and Derbyshire were brought to Annesley Sidings where they were made up into trainloads for the next leg of their journey as far as Woodford, from which place they would be sent on to London or elsewhere according to needs. Once the fuel had been discharged the collieries were anxious to refill the trucks as soon as possible thus producing a corresponding northbound flow of empties no less important to the customer than the original consignment, and these workings could be guaranteed to raise the echoes as they accelerated through the station to tackle the ensuing incline.

Commodities other than coal were conveyed by the fast goods trains, ranging from plate steel from Dorman Long and other producers on Tees-side destined for South Wales, through fish from Hull and Grimsby leaving behind its own distinctive smell, to general merchandise carried by such trains as the Swindon to York express goods, known generally as "The Rabbits". Just prior to nationalisation the LNER revolutionised the mineral workings between Annesley and Woodford by improving the service of loose coupled trains between these places. Engines and men from Annesley were involved and worked to Woodford and back within their 8 hour shift. On arrival at Woodford the loco was taken on shed to be serviced, whilst a freshly prepared engine was given to the Annesley crew for the return working. These trains were operated under the strict rule that if they could not leave Annesley Yards on time they were cancelled, and the men could be sent home, thereby losing pay.

LNER Class B8 4-6-0s took on some of the earliest workings, but the Woodfords which were soon monopolised by the GC 2-8-0s rebuilt to Class 01 acquired the nickname of "Windcutters" in railway circles. At one time all but 5 of the 58 engines rebuilt to Class 01 were allocated to Annesley, but good as they were, their performance was bettered by that most excellent BR design, the Class 9F, thirty of these finding their way to this shed, where they were well received.

The closure of Mapperley Tunnel due to the effects of mineworkings, which has been referred to elsewhere, necessitated the diversion of GN section goods and mineral trains through Victoria and so brought an increase in the quantity and variety of freight passing through. However, the declining years had arrived and with one branch service after the other being withdrawn, then the wholesale closure for local passengers of the line to Sheffield on 4th March 1963, the station fell into rapid decline. Former LNER engines appeared less frequently, and although the 9Fs remained for a time, it was the former LMS types which held sway. Class 8Fs replaced W.D. and other eight coupled classes, the Royal Scots had their fling on the disgraceful Nottingham to Marylebone trains which were offered to the travelling public, followed by the Britannia interlude, but all the time the ubiquitous Black Fives were taking over so that when the end came, to all intents and purposes, in September 1966 these engines had the field to themselves. It suffered a lingering death, and in the final days Victoria was neglected and forlorn, but it had been a truly great station.

134. Victoria. A very smartly turned out Class C12 No. 4016 stands at the end of No. 5 bay platform and manages to get in the way to some degree of the main feature of the photograph which is the staired access at Parliament Street. Many people found this exit more convenient according to where they wanted to be in the city. No office existed at this point, and therefore only those with return or season tickets would enter the station this way. With the development of new shop premises the Parliament Street entrance did not stay the full course being closed on 23.4.59 and removed shortly afterwards. *Photo: J.F. Henton*

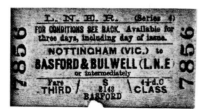

135. Victoria, c.1956. A busy scene caught by the camera from the Parliament Street footbridge with an empty mineral train doubtless bound for Annesley occupying platform 4 as one of the famed Annesley–Woodford 'Windcutters' heads south along platform 7 line with Class 01 No. 63630 typifying the external condition of most of Annesley's engines. At platform 10 V2 No. 60815 has charge of an up express, whilst the bay platforms are occupied respectively by J39 No. 64832 and J6 No. 64230.
Photo: J. Cupit

MARKET RASEN STEEPLECHASES — FIRST RACE 2.30 pm. LAST RACE 5.0 pm.

TO

MARKET RASEN AND CLEETHORPES

EASTER MONDAY 18th APRIL 1960

FROM	TIMES OF DEPARTURE	RETURN FARES Second Class to		ARRIVAL TIMES ON RETURN
		Market Rasen	Clee-thorpes	
	am	s d	s d	pm
NOTTINGHAM Victoria	8 40			10 20
NEW BASFORD	8 46			10 14
BULWELL COMMON	8 52	10/-	13/-	10 7
HUCKNALL Central	8 59			10 0
KIRKBY-IN-ASHFIELD Central	9 13			9 47
SUTTON-IN-ASHFIELD Central	9 19			9 39
MANSFIELD Central	9 30	9/6		9 27
	am			pm
MARKET RASEN arrive	10 45	Passengers return same day at		8 16
CLEETHORPES	11 51			7 15

ACCOMMODATION STRICTLY LIMITED — PLEASE BOOK IN ADVANCE

CHILDREN under three years of age, free ; three years and under fourteen, half-fares ; fractions of 1d. to be reckoned as 1d.
CONDITIONS OF ISSUE
These tickets are issued subject to the British Transport Commission's published Regulations and Conditions applicable to British Railways, exhibited at their Stations or obtainable free of charge at Station Booking Offices.
For LUGGAGE ALLOWANCES also see these Regulations and Conditions.
RAIL TICKETS CAN BE OBTAINED IN ADVANCE AT STATIONS AND OFFICIAL RAILWAY AGENTS
Further information will be supplied on application to Stations, Official Railway Agents, or to H. BULLOUGH, District Commercial Manager, DERBY. Telephone: Derby 42441, Extn. 204.

March, 1960   BR 35000

LONDON MIDLAND   Arthur Geunt & Sons (Printers) Ltd. Heanor Derbyshire

136. Victoria, c.1960. Class 04 No. 63644 wheels a coal train under Parliament Street and briefly out into the open before entering Thurland Street tunnel where the line reverted to double track, and effectively comprised a bottleneck at the south end of the station. The daylight beyond the tunnel marks Weekday Cross Junction, but take pity on the poor signalman on duty in Nottingham Victoria South box, who was obliged to work in the gloom below one of the city's busiest street. *Photo: J.S. Hayes*

137. Victoria, c.1949. Standing on the most westerly through line by a mixed rake of vans is Colwick's Class K2 No. 61723 sporting the earliest BR tender style of painting. Colwick found much work for its stud of Moguls, and they were regularly seen on excursions to the Lincolnshire coast, keeping them going seven days a week. *Photo: J.F. Henton*

138. Victoria, c.1958. Many of the passenger diagrams were so arranged that Nottingham was merely an intermediate stop, the example here being a Grantham to Derby Friargate train hauled by Class J6 No. 64248. Some of Colwick's engines were outstationed at Derby where a sub-shed was provided, and which covered workings out to Stafford and Burton-on-Trent. *Photo: Author's collection*

139. Victoria, c.1938. Class B7 No. 5469 is a member of the most numerous class of 4-6-0 designed by the GCR. These 4 cylinder types were used throughout the system and were the nearest thing possessed by the GCR to a mixed traffic locomotive, finding much employment on fast goods and excursion traffic, as well as taking their turns on the cross country expresses. In terms of fuel consumption they have been often criticised, but for haulage capacity they had the edge when compared with their stablemates. No. 5469 will take forward the 1.55pm for South Wales. *Photo: J.F. Henton*

BOOKING OF SEATS
TO HOLIDAY RESORTS

SUMMER 1960

SEATS MAY BE BOOKED FROM—

NOTTINGHAM VICTORIA
DERBY FRIARGATE
MANSFIELD CENTRAL
ILKESTON NORTH
HUCKNALL CENTRAL

AND CERTAIN OTHER STATIONS
ON THE TRAINS SHOWN OVERLEAF

FEE **1/-** PER SEAT

UNDER THESE ARRANGEMENTS PASSENGERS ARE ASSURED OF A NUMBERED SEAT BUT CHOICE OF SEAT, I.E. CORNER, FACING, OR BACK TO ENGINE CANNOT BE GUARANTEED. **NORMAL SEAT RESERVATIONS (FEE 2/-) DO NOT APPLY BY THESE TRAINS.**

RETURN ARRANGEMENTS
SEATS CAN ALSO BE BOOKED UNDER A SIMILAR ARRANGEMENT AT THE FEE OF 1/- ON RETURN TRAINS FROM SKEGNESS MABLETHORPE AND SUTTON-ON-SEA ON APPLICATION TO THE STATION MASTER AT THE APPROPRIATE STATION.

Seats may be booked on personal or postal application to the Station Master at the Stations named or to any station or authorised ticket agency. Bookings will close at 5.0 p.m. on the Wednesday prior to the date of travel. Postal application, stating train, destination, class and date of travel should be accompanied by the appropriate fee and stamped addressed envelope. When seats are booked for children under three years of age, half-fare rail tickets must be held.

SEATS CANNOT BE BOOKED BY TELEPHONE

The British Transport Commission will undertake only the booking of seats, berths and other accommodation on the condition that, if from any cause, such accommodation is not booked they shall refund any sum which may have been paid by the passenger for such booking and shall not incur any liability for their failure to provide it.

LONDON MIDLAND

From NOTTINGHAM Victoria

TRAIN	PERIOD OF OPERATION		DESTINATION
11.24 pm FO	17th June—8th July and 2nd and 9th September		PORTSMOUTH
10.55 pm FO	15th July—26th August inclusive		PORTSMOUTH
12.45 am SO	18th June—3rd September	"	RAMSGATE
1.0 am SO	2nd July—27th August	"	HASTINGS
5.56 am SO	2nd July—3rd September	"	LLANDUDNO
6.21 am SO	18th June—3rd September	"	LIVERPOOL
7.16 am SO	18th June—10th September	"	YARMOUTH
6.44 am SO	9th July—27th August	"	YARMOUTH
8.5 am SO	2nd July—10th September	"	SKEGNESS
8.15 am SO	18th June—10th September	"	MABLETHORPE
8.28 am SO	18th and 25th June, 2nd July, 27th August and 3rd September		SCARBOROUGH
8.40 am SO	18th June—10th September inclusive		LONDON Marylebone
9.7 am SO	9th July—20th August		SCARBOROUGH
9.12 am SO	18th June—10th September	"	MABLETHORPE
9.30 am SO	18th June—10th September	"	SKEGNESS
11.48 am SO	18th June—10th September	"	SKEGNESS

From DERBY Friargate

*11.35 pm FO	17th June—2nd September inclusive		RAMSGATE
*6.15 am SO	18th June—10th September	"	YARMOUTH
*6.52 am SO	2nd July—3rd September	"	LLANDUDNO
*7.30 am SO	18th June—10th September	"	SKEGNESS
*9.25 am SO	18th June—10th September	"	MABLETHORPE
*10.50 am SO	18th June—10th September	"	SKEGNESS

*Reservations also from ILKESTON North and KIMBERLEY on these trains.

From BASFORD North

†6.40 am SO	18th June—10th September inclusive		SKEGNESS
†6.50 am SO	18th June—10th September	"	MABLETHORPE
†9.15 am SO	9th July—20th August	"	SCARBOROUGH

†Reservations also from BULWELL COMMON, HUCKNALL Central, KIRKBY-IN-ASHFIELD Central, SUTTON-IN-ASHFIELD Central and MANSFIELD Central on these trains.

From MANSFIELD Central

‡5.53 am SO	9th July—17th August inclusive		YARMOUTH

‡Reservations also from SUTTON-IN-ASHFIELD Central, KIRKBY-IN-ASHFIELD Central, HUCKNALL Central and BULWELL COMMON on this train.

SO—Saturdays only.   FO—Fridays only.

February 1960   **LONDON MIDLAND**   Arthur Gaunt & Sons (Printers) Ltd., Heanor, Derbyshire.   BR 35001

140. Victoria, c.1960. Surely nobody who used the station could ever forget these signboards adjacent to the footbridge on platforms 7 and 10, the up through lines. Combined with the efforts of the station announcer whose distinctive voice over the tannoy system rolling off the intermediate stops (e.g. calling at Loughborough, Leicester, Rugby, Woodford Halse, Banbury etc.) as if it were second nature, these signs ensured that it was virtually impossible to get on the wrong train. In all probability the whole thing perished by fire but what an attractive item it would have provided for the National Railway Museum if only someone with foresight had been present at the critical moment.

Photo: E.N.C. Haywood

141. Victoria, c.1949. A stopping train for Leicester emerges briefly into the sunlight before traversing Thurland Street tunnel powered by Class D10 No.2654 *Walter Burgh Gair*, the name being that of a director of the GCR. Note the colour light signal with ancillary platform indicator, displaying useful information to the driver of an approaching train and allowing plenty of time to apply the brake especially if signalled into one of the bays.

Photo: J.F. Henton

142. Victoria, c.1927. Class C1 Atlantic No. 3295 of Sheffield Neepsend shed heads north with one of the cross country express trains for which the GCR line was noted, the first three vehicles of which are GWR clerestory coaches. This train could have been the 'Ports to Ports' express running between Barry and Newcastle.

Photo: Author's collection

143. Victoria, c.1931. Although the GCR main line saw very little use of diesel railcars in the BR period it should not be forgotten that the LNER found employment for steam railcars locally, as evidenced by No. 45 *Commerce* showing off the apple green and cream paintwork adopted by that company, and also used on the tourist coaching stock. What a pity this is not a colour photograph. They worked on the ex. GNR routes, for example to Basford via Gedling, and also some Shirebrook services.

Photo: Author's collection

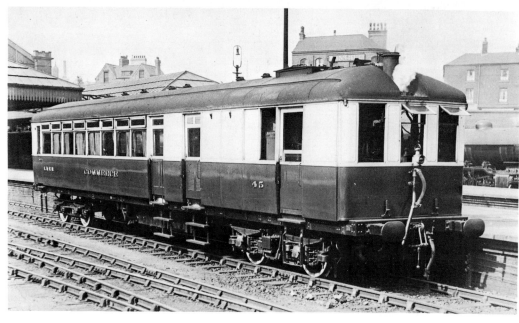

144. Victoria, 26th September 1955. On a delightfully sunny afternoon one of the 58 Thompson rebuilds of the indigenous GCR 2-8-0s, No. 63890 emerges from Mansfield Road tunnel and heads south with a train for Woodford. Much trouble was encountered at Nottinghamshire engine sheds due to excessive lime content in the water, and although water softening plants were provided, and even tablets to feed into the tender tanks, the problem would not go away, and the external appearance of an Annesley resident with the resultant white deposit clinging to the boiler cladding was quite typical. But external appearance is sometimes misleading; Annesley men were keen and for many years they operated the Woodford 'out and home' turns with great success. *Photo: J.F. Henton*

145. Victoria, 31st May 1951. This is the epitome of `Nottingham Vic'. For those who knew it no further comment is necessary; for those who didn't just pause here awhile and Mr. Haywood's picture will almost come to life. For the record the goods train is held at the signal half way along the platform because the 5.50pm to Pinxton is about to leave ahead of it. *Photo: E.C. Haywood*

146. Victoria. North Eastern Railway engines were no strangers to the LNER lines around Nottingham as evidenced by Class B16 No. 922 heading north with an unfitted goods train. York engines reached Annesley daily where sometimes they were 'borrowed' and put to work on whatever duty was required of them. If a foreign locomotive was unable to take up its normal return working back home, Annesley would have to use one of its own allocation, or, more likely, being a sub-shed to Colwick, the latter would be expected to provide a substitute. The foreigner would then be repaired and, often as not, available for traffic at a time when no suitable return working was immediately due, so it would be put to good use on one of Annesley's own diagrams, and it could be a week or more before it was restored to its own depot. York also sent B1s and V2s, but it was always a pleasure to see the different outlines of a NER design on one of the fitted goods trains, and more rarely on an express.

*Photo: T.G. Hepburn/
Author's collection*

147. Victoria, 13th May 1962. In the post war era many a steam special included Nottingham in its itinerary. The East Midlands branch of the Railway Correspondence & Travel Society had an excellent reputation for devising interesting and inexpensive railtours, often with unusual engines, and these ran regularly in the 1950s and 1960s. The Society adopted the Southern Railway 'Schools' class No. 30925 *Cheltenham* as its symbol and borrowed it for the day to assist Class 2P No. 40646 on one such tour to Darlington. The locomotives were prepared for this duty at Annesley shed, probably the first time these strange types had been seen, and while they had possession of it they used the SR engine on the Hotchley Hill pilot trip fetching the gypsum traffic from the Gotham branch. Was this the oddest diagram worked by the Schools class?

Photo: J.F Henton

148. Victoria, 29th February 1958. One of the best known of the cross country trains running on the GCR lines was the York–Bournemouth which somehow managed to survive until the end of through express workings on this route, latterly hauled by a Type 3 diesel (Class 37) from Sheffield. This was the only express train worthy of the name which operated on the GCR line diesel powered, but in this illustration it draws into platform 7 composed of the familiar green SR stock, therefore a daily appearance, hauled by Class B1 No. 61066, itself no stranger to the area.

Photo: J.F. Henton

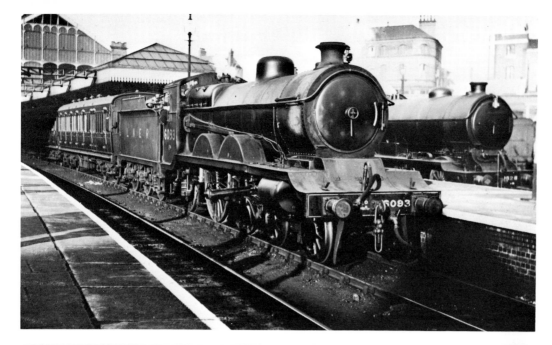

149. Victoria. Robinson designed Atlantic No. 6093 takes charge of a local passenger train probably bound for Leicester awaiting departure from one of the south end bays. Despite one or two LNER modifications applied in the name of standardisation, the handsome appearance of this GCR thoroughbred cannot be denied. The fact that they only rarely strayed from their native line bears testimony to their more than satisfactory performance.

Photo: J.F Henton

150. Victoria, c.1937. The 3 cylinder Class B17 of the 'Footballer' series were allocated in large numbers to the GCR line in the 1930s, replacing to a great extent the Robinson Atlantics so beloved of the top link drivers at Leicester shed who had a large share of the express workings. For a time these Gresley designed 4-6-0s were the principal engines used on Marylebone and the many cross-country services; they were not universally liked partly because their riding qualities did not match up to the Atlantics and Directors which had coped well with the modest loads and tight schedules, the hallmark of GCR practice. However, in the years leading up to the outbreak of war train loads increased appreciably and even the B17s struggled to keep time on occasions, being themselves superseded by Gresley Pacifics and V2s, the latter being particularly suited to the passenger and fast goods workings. Some B17s remained in the area until after the war, but all eventually left for depots in East Anglia, the last ones going from Colwick who often rostered them to the Mansfield and Edwinstowe stopping trains. *Photo: Author's collection*

151. Nottingham, Victoria, c.1940. War time departure for the South from Platform 10 as class V2 No. 4831 *Durham School* resplendent in LNER apple green livery eases forward past the watchful eye of a member of the local defence volunteers, complete with rifle (or is it just a dummy?). Although V2's were domestic to the Great Central Line this particular engine was stranger being based in the North East. By no means certain, it is thought that the train is destined for the Western region via Banbury and it could be a troop special. Most of the scheduled cross country trains used platform 7. Whilst locomotive and rolling stock are commendably clean and, viewed from the air, the roofs of the coaches would surely have made an easy target for an enemy bomber, in 1940 things were only just beginning to hot up and at the date of this photograph the terrible bombing raids on Sheffield, Coventry and other cities are perhaps still in the planning stages. The trolleys in the siding suggest that some engineering work was scheduled in the area.

Photo: T.G. Hepburn

152. Victoria, c.1952. At the opening of the station in 1900 the GNR to a large extent abandoned for passenger use its terminus at London Road. Not so the LNWR however, whose trains continued to use that station until May 1944. The Northampton trains ceased in December 1953 and here Northampton based Class 2P No. 40522 occupies platform 11 on the 6.25pm service back home, its tender still bearing the letters L.M.S.

Photo: J.F. Henton

L. N. E. R.
FOR CONDITIONS SEE BACK. Available for three days, including day of issue.

1941

NOTTINGHAM (VICTORIA) to
KIMBERLEY for WATNALL
NUTTALL & GILTBROOK

Fare / S 1s.0½d.C
THIRD / 2143 \ CLASS
KIMBERLEY for W. N. & C

153. Victoria, c.1959. The signal box at Nottingham Victoria North was unique in design, its overhanging full gable roof atop the slimline brick building being made necessary by the convergence of all tracks into the tunnel which was double track only. In this illustration the nameboard carries the correct name, but this was later changed to an enamel version worded "Victoria North". In pre-grouping days, the three shift box, open continuously, was worked by two GNR and one GCR grade assisted by a train register lad, whilst at the other end of the station the South Box had the same arrangement in reverse thus ensuring that at all times the extremities were signalled by men from different companies. *Photo: G.H. Platt*

154. Victoria, 19th September 1955. The Eastern Region of BR chose the Grantham to Nottingham line for some of the earliest of their DMU services. This new form of motive power soon took over the local trains in the West Riding and dominated the scene in Lincolnshire, but made no great impact on the stopping trains using Victoria. Here a two car set stands ready to leave for Grantham on the first day of diesel operation.

155. Nottingham, Victoria, 23rd May 1958. Turn the clock back to the 1920's and you may well have seen this locomotive proudly heading one of the Marylebone to Manchester Expresses which the Director type handled with great distinction. Treading the same path but many years later the class D11 No. 62662 *Prince of Wales* has a much easier assignment with a return stopping train to Sheffield calling at most stations including some on the Chesterfield loop line and after stabling the coaches it will retire to its home shed of Darnall to wait for another easy day's work. Some of the coaching stock seems to be from the Thompson era no longer constructed of teak. The driver is justly proud of his well groomed steed, a delight to the eyes as its paintwork shines in the afternoon sunlight. Sheffield Darnall was home to the Director class in their last years and during the week they found employment on the local trains as far south as Leicester but at weekends they were very popular with the excursions from the Nottinghamshire and Derbyshire mining villages to the East Coast Resorts. *Prince of Wales* alas did not survive the cutters torch but fortunately one of her contemporaries *Butler Henderson* is preserved in working order on the Great Central Railway running in preserved fashion from Loughborough.   *Photo: J.P. Wilson*

156. Nottingham, Victoria, n.d. One of Mr Robinson's outstandingly successful goods engines No. 5380 draws to a halt by the water crane on platform 7 ready to spend the next few minutes replenishing its tank. It is well known that vast numbers of these locomotives were built to the same basic design for use by the Railway Operating Department in the First World War and thereafter many were stored around the country rusting away for long periods. The government of the day hoped to recoup their outlay by selling off the surplus locomotives rather than having to scrap them but in many cases they had a long wait, the locomotives lying idle until the price was right. The London and North Western Railway and the Great Western Railway had purchased some but eventually it was the LNER which became the owner of most of them and it was not until 1927 that they completed their deals with the government. Most required overhaul and some were re-boilered by the LNER and later into British Railways days thus ensuring that maximum use was obtained from them over a long period. The first few wagons bear the name of their owners and they had to be kept in satisfactory condition particularly as far as lubrication was concerned in order to work on the main lines. They are headed in this case by one of the engines actually built for the Great Central Railway. The buildings in the background are on Glasshouse Street, the one to the right displaying the name of one of Nottingham's most famous brewers Messrs Shipstones. To the rear of that building on Huntingdon Street could be found Nottingham's indoor market, now, as with the station, long gone and much lamented. Teak coaches stand in the bay platform for the use of third class passengers.   *Photo: Author's collection*

157. Nottingham, Victoria, c.1963. In the dying years of the Great Central line LMS Black 5s were common-place and, sad to say, most of them appeared in a deplorable condition. On this occasion however Leicester Central shed certainly has made some effort with No. 44690 standing on five coaches at platform 10 with a stopping train probably originating at Sheffield and going only as far as Leicester. By this date the continued passage of goods and passenger trains including those diverted from the former GN Lines following the closure of the Mapperley Tunnel, taken together with natural accumulation of grime, left the station ready for a second post war cleaning which it would never receive.

Photo: V. Forster

158. Victoria, c.1964. Perhaps the only place outside London where locomotives from all four English Regions of British Railways could be seen daily was Oxford. Because of its connection with the Western Region at Banbury the GC line saw daily scheduled operation of ex GWR engines as far as Leicester, but any which penetrated further north was by way of exception. The station was already dying when this photograph was taken but it could still conjure up a remarkable array of motive power, all engines on this occasion coming within the mixed traffic category. The B1 No. 61092 and Western Region 'Hall' No. 6911 *Holker Hall* occupy centre stage but these are framed discreetly by an LMS Black 5 to the right whilst a Britannia standing at platform 10 just gets a look in.

Photo: Author's collection

159. Victoria, c.1968. "They've torn up the loop and there's only a scar to show where the water crane stood". These words taken from a Dave Goulder ballad seem appropriate to this scene of destruction. Gone are the demolition contractors and the site is ready for the builders with their cranes and cement mixers to take over. Very soon this corner of the city will be transformed beyond recognition to form the Victoria Shopping Centre and flats, the basement area comprising a car park and goods delivery areas for the shops above. Dave Goulder, one time fireman at Kirkby sheds, wrote several songs about railwaymen, most of them with reference to his home depot or to some incident well recalled such as the day Class 8F No. 48073 finished up "parked at forty five degrees" in the turntable pit. This and other gems were considered good enough by the BBC who produced an album of Dave's songs in the late 1960s entitled "Green All The Way".

Photo: Author's collection

160. Weekday Cross Junction, c.1948. Until the BR five figure numbering system had been fully worked out, newly built locomotives to former LNER designs were put into traffic with four figure numbers prefixed by the letter E as depicted by this example No. E 1298 built by the North British Locomotive Company in Glasgow in March 1948 sporting the green passenger livery and carrying its number on the front buffer beam in characteristic LNER style. The train is one of empty coaching stock which will be going no further than Queen's Road Carriage Sidings. Attention is drawn to the use of white discs in preference to lamps to display the head code, the B.1 Class being provided with electric headlights which meant that a fixed lamp was to be found in each of the four positions on the front of the locomotive. Obviously during the hours of daylight it would be impossible to see which lamps were illuminated therefore white discs were used for a few years but these soon gave way to white headlamps fixed to brackets located above the electric light positions. The main exception to this was the continued use of the white discs in East Anglia until the demise of steam on ex GER lines. The footsteps of Garner's Hill leading up towards High Pavement may just be glimpsed beyond the retaining wall to the right of the tracks whilst those of Middle Hill are seen more clearly to the left of the picture. All the buildings have since been demolished but a small pleasantly landscaped park exists replacing the factory building on the right. The retaining wall above the signal does remain with fading traces of old advertments appearing on its north elevation. Today's visitor to this corner of Nottingham will still find much to admire architecturally along High Pavement, and in the area around the old Lace Market and some of the buildings on Thurland Street beneath which the train has just passed are well worth seeing. *Photo: J.F. Henton*

161. Weekday Cross, 16th November, c.1962. There is still a Dolcis shoe shop in Nottingham but not the one shown here because all the shops in the foreground had to be cleared to make way for the present day Broadmarsh Centre, a new road and a multi storey car park. No longer does the brown and cream bus operated by West Bridgford Urban District Council take people to Musters Road, and, looking across the old rooftops from a westerly viewpoint a Class 9F hurrying its train of empty mineral wagons to expectant collieries is just another scene from the past. The train is approaching the signal box at Weekday Cross Junction where the line from Colwick trails in to its right and makes a connection before plunging into the smoke and gloom of Thurland Street tunnel. The factory appearing in illustration 160 stands prominently in front of the spired church, the latter no longer having an ecclesiastical use but with masonry cleaned and restored it is now a tourist attraction as Nottingham Lace Centre. The square tower of St. Mary's Church in the Lace market is not quite so tall and continues to seek the attendance of worshippers more so than tourists. *Photo: Author's collection/J.F. Henton*

162. Weekday Cross, 4th May 1958. This view along the main line is from the bridge adjacent to Weekday Cross signal box. Note the standard GC cast iron bridge number plate to the left.

163. Weekday Cross Junction. Standing between and thereby separating the lines to Grantham and those to Leicester was the typical Great Central style signal box, its name board informing us that this was Weekday Cross Junction. Here to the south of Thurland Street Tunnel, but only just so, four generations of signalmen found work in this continuously open box and both protected and diverted trains accordingly. Looking out of the open window the man on duty would be able to see the next cabin along the line at Nottingham Victoria South assuming of course that all the smoke had escaped. The cast iron signal adjacent to the bridge post warns drivers coming from the Grantham Line of a speed restriction to 10 miles per hour over the points.

Save for the provision of four through running lines in each direction at Nottingham Victoria Station the section of line 2 miles 43 chains in length between Bagthorpe Junction and Weekday Cross Junction, most of it in tunnel and on a rising gradient northbound was double track and saw intensive use. In the LNER era and until severe mining subsidence problems closed Mapperley Tunnel as from the 4th of April 1960, the GN Line domestic freight traffic from its Derbyshire Lines avoided this already busy section of line. However in the late 1950's many of the coal trains and those taking iron ore to the Stanton Works at Ilkeston were diverted from Colwick via Weekday Cross Junction increasing the intensity of use once more. A special section of the working timetable for 1927 gives running times of all booked trains, excluding light engines, between the two points and merits careful study. Approximately 200 trains run in each direction in 24 hours, each passenger train stopping in section at least once. In the up direction the first train after midnight was the 11.45pm mineral from Annesley to Woodford passing Bagthorpe Junction at 12.06am and being allowed 11 minutes to passing Weekday Cross Junction. The first five hours saw the passage of several such trains destined for Woodford all with the uniform allowance of 11 minutes over the section of line under consideration. Save for Monday mornings this initial period saw only 2 passenger trains departing from Victoria at 12.33am and 1.17am destined respectively for Bristol and Marylebone. Several express goods occupied the line during the small hours notably the 9.15pm from Dewsnap to London and the 7.20pm the previous evening from Stairfoot to Banbury Junction. The local passenger service got off the mark with a rather strange working originating at Basford North, spending 3 minutes at Victoria then forming the 5.06am departure for Pinxton via Weekday Cross and Daybrook. By 7 o'clock the more important class B goods workings had come and gone, these being allowed 10 minutes from passing Bagthorpe Junction to passing Weekday Cross.

Fascinating though it is considerations of space do not permit reproduction of 8 foolscap pages to show the complete summary of up and down trains through this particular bottleneck but we can pause to consider the busy period between noon and 2.00pm. The two most important trains on the down line were the Banbury to Marshgate return fish empties and the through train from Southampton to Newcastle, the latter forming the

1 o'clock departure from Victoria. Going the opposite way at 12.14 was the Manchester to Marylebone Express which carried the through coaches from Bradford and Huddersfield added to the train at Sheffield Victoria. Three minutes after this departure a Doncaster based GN Atlantic hauling 3 coaches slipped into the station. Two of these vehicles, one being a brake, would appear in LNER teak, stark contrast to the third which sported Southern Railway green. The following day the roles would be reversed on this interesting lightweight train which originated at Leeds. Nottingham was not the ultimate goal for these vehicles which were on the move again in less than 20 minutes, attached now to the through Newcastle to Bournemouth Express which came from York by way of the Swinton and Knottingly joint line to gain ex-Great Central metals and which in later years was headed by the LMS engine from Lowmoor Shed, Bradford, which had yielded at Sheffield the through coaches from its own city and Huddersfield previously referred to. The Bournemouth train with its increased load left at 12.36 whilst the GN Atlantic just referred to turned to retrace its steps later.

The next hour or so saw much activity with the arrival and departure of local passenger services and some movement of empty coaching stock but there was time to fit in one of the class A goods trains not stopping within the bottleneck and passing Weekday Cross 12.48. This was the steel train from Scunthorpe to the Great Western Railway via Banbury Junction. Towards the end of the 2 hour period the up line saw the arrival at 1.51pm of the express passenger train from Newcastle to Swansea, this time treating spectators to the sight of chocolate and cream coaches whose wheels were moving again in no more than 4 minutes following a change of engine.

Unlike its counterpart at the northern end of the bottleneck the junction at Weekday Cross was flat. The few minutes either side of the shift change at 2 o'clock saw several trains passing Weekday Cross which, if they were all travelling exactly to time, meant the signalman was busy with point and signal levers, block instruments and making entries in the train register but all would be well. However, it only required a tardy passenger to hold up the local train from Radcliffe-on-Trent for one minute, say at Netherfield, and that would cause the signalman to hesitate before allowing it a clear road into Victoria, for that might delay the 1.55pm to South Wales. If the signalman did not give priority to the local and if it happened also to be a Saturday then the local might have to wait for the Leicester to Nottingham passenger train due in Victoria at 1.59pm before getting a clear road. On the other hand of course if the 1.55pm itself was running a little late that might well interfere with the light engine from Colwick shed booked to work the 2.24pm departure (Saturdays excepted) or alternatively the 2.05pm arrival from Chesterfield Market Place via Shirebrook North, the Leen Valley lines and the Nottingham Suburban Railway. Obviously control would be in touch with the signalman to advise any severe late running but if it were only a matter of minutes then the signalman's own initiative would be relied upon.

Photo: D.H. Beecroft

164. Weekday Cross, n.d. In the twilight years of the Great Central Line the Marylebone trains were hardly worthy of the title 'express' and were therefore invariably referred to as being 'semi-fast'. As in the first years loads were light but there the comparison ends for BR Standard 5 No. 73156 had an easy schedule to maintain. By now this was the forgotten line which did not feature in BR modernisation plans being regarded as something of a liability. As contemporary passengers will testify all the energies of the authorities at the time were channelled towards dissuasion, what with dirty coaches, poor facilities, pedestrian schedules and the odd engine failure thrown in for good measure.

Many steep passages and alleyways were to be found in the Broadmarsh area of the city and this feature has enabled Don Beecroft to capture on film something of the atmosphere of the early 60's with the train gathering speed as it rattles over the points at Weekday Cross.
Photo: D.H. Beecroft

165. Arkwright Street. Early 1930s. This view looking towards the city is taken from the down platform where some thought had gone into the provision of an extended canopy. Commuters arriving on the up side would be keen to get to their places of work but at the end of their labours they had the relative comfort, especially on a rainy day, of being protected by this canopy whilst awaiting the arrival of the stopping train which would speed them towards their homes. The platforms themselves are of generous width doubtless to cater for the surge of morning and evening travellers. Certainly the down platform had to accommodate a copious amount of material once in each 24 hours when most of the city was asleep. London newspapers arrived before 5 o'clock on the famous train which for many years left Marylebone at 2.32am, and which required of engine and crew alike, work of the best quality in order to keep time. As it screeched to a halt the parcels van doors would fly open and one after the other packs of newspapers, pre-labelled to various destinations and bound with string, would be loaded on barrows in a frantic rush which can best be described as, organised chaos. Waiting in Arkwright Street below were the vans required to take these heavy packages to all parts of the city. The loading process was quickened considerably by the use of two metal spiral chutes connecting the down platform with the gloomy hallway below. Arkwright Street, being conveniently located for some manufacturing industries attracted a respectable amount of parcels traffic, much of which was heavy and, as one railway worker stationed here said, "Handling the newspapers was a darned sight easier than dealing with outgoing parcels". The nameboard on the left is in two portions, the upper one being replaced in later years by an enamel board excluding the word 'Nottingham'. This station was also geographically the nearest to Trent Bridge and the full wording on the lower board reads, "Nearest station to Trent Bridge cricket and football grounds".

Photo: D. Thompson

166. Arkwright Street. c.1969. The unusual view point brings into prominence the lift shafts located at the northerly end of its station. For more years than one cares to say the famous newspaper train left Marylebone in the early hours and cut a dash through the night, pulling up sharply here to off load its urgent freight which would then be immediately disgorged into the shute. Very definitely the quickest means of getting it to waiting vehicles in the street below. Any consignment starting its journey here of course had to be got up to the platform and that operation was decidedly more labour intensive. *Photo: M.A. King*

167. (Above-left) Arkwright Street, 8th March 1969. Situated in that part of the city called The Meadows, Arkwright Street Station was obliged for a short time to play the role of being the main GCR station in the city. Passenger services on the London Extension commenced in 1899 but until the 24th May 1900, Victoria Station was not sufficiently complete to be ready for use. Thereafter its importance dwindled considerably as a passenger station, all the expresses and indeed most of the local services thundering through. The public entrance on Waterway Street as shown here could hardly have been less conspicuous being virtually a single doorway leading to a staircase which gave access to the elevated platforms. Again, towards the end of its career it achieved some importance when Victoria Station closed its doors for the last time and formed the northern terminus of the Nottingham to Rugby service operated by diesel railcars from 1967 until they expired on 5th May 1969. No expense has been spared by BR who went to the trouble of providing a new style sign above the entrance, although most of the people using the Rugby trains were regulars and may not even have noticed it. *Photo: M.A. King*

168. (Above-right) Queens Walk, c.1988. Queens Walk was at one time a road, but nowadays where it is fronted by the former goods offices, it is appropriately enough, a pedestrian way – if one overlooks the existence of a cycle track. Many slums have been cleared away from this area of Nottingham and an extensive development of houses and flats has been undertaken by the Council, with the result that in almost every case, the former routes of streets and alleys have been built upon. To those who knew the area in the 1950s, this part of the Meadows is a puzzling maze of Courts and Closes. However, in the middle of all this the old GCR Goods Offices have survived, the external brickwork cleaned to improve its appearance, and for some time past has been used as a Community Centre. As this photograph confirms, the result is a handsome building surrounded by established trees, a welcome change from the monotonous architecture of the younger dwellings. This is the western elevation, but to the rear of the building a car park has been provided, which faces the eastern wall which has suffered a different treatment about which the least said the better. *Photo: W. Taylor*

169. (Below) Arkwright Street, 15th May 1954. Six coaches and a van provide no excessive task for Class B1 No. 61096 as it heads through Arkwright Street Station giving the passengers an elevated view across the Meadows with two and three storey Victorian tenements crowding the line on both sides.

170. Queens Walk, c.1957. Not an aerial view, but nonetheless interesting is this view taken from the top of the goods warehouse looking down on a northbound express hauled by typical GC line motive power in the shape of V2 No. 60837. To the right of the train are the goods lines stretching out of sight towards the Trent, the down line being served by a parachute style water crane, better to put the "bag" in here than cluttering up the works in Victoria Station. The signal set at danger protects the exit from the goods yard itself, the main layout of which is to the west of the through lines, although some cattle pens were sited on the opposite side. As can be gauged from the position of the wagons in the yard, its level was below that of the main line giving rise to the existence of the lengthy retaining wall in the foreground. Beyond the main lines further sidings accommodate both passenger and parcels vehicles and in the distance the sorry remains of the elevated coaling stage of Arkwright Street Motive Power Depot can be made out. It is evident from the extent of the development that the GCR meant to have a large slice of the traffic which Nottingham produced and received.
Photo: C.A. Hill

171. Arkwright Street Shed, 14th July 1935. The shed was located on the east side of the main line opposite to the Queens Walk Goods Warehouse and was brought into use in March 1899, its design being standard with other London Extension depots such as Annesley and Leicester although Arkwright Street was a scaled down version having four roads, sufficient to accommodate engines for the passenger and fast goods workings. The roof was the familiar saw-tooth profile of a north light design and the shedmasters office was strategically placed, its bay window affording the incumbent a clear view across the locomotive yard. Although the building survived and was put to good use until well into the BR period, it ceased to operate as a motive power depot in the full sense as long ago as 1909, reputedly on account of the high water rates charged by Nottingham Corporation. From that year most of the staff and locomotive allocation were transferred to Annesley, some of the passenger turns being taken on by Leicester shed. For a while the longer distance express goods trains running out of Queens Walk were covered by crews who signed for duty at the shed but in later years even these became Annesley's province; leaving only a few pilot duties to cover. Visiting engines still called here to take on coal and water but with ample room to spare Arkwright Street was used to store engines temporarily taken out of traffic, a practice which continued till about 1950. Towards the end the whole area became overgrown and weed-ridden, the 54' turntable being salvaged for use elsewhere, but oddly enough, the raised coalstage, the sandfurnace house and even the clock over the shed entrance soldiered on to the last. At least three visiting engines are on shed, no doubt awaiting their turn on braked goods trains, including K3 No.1141 and 4 cylinder B7 No.5032 directly behind it.
Photo: W.A. Camwell

172. Queens Walk, May 1949. The story of train services on the Great Central line in the BR era is one of decline, at first steady, but later under the auspices of LM Region control, quicker by degree. No evidence of this here, on the contrary, this splendid sight must have cheered the hearts of railwaymen and passengers alike. Looking at the train you may be forgiven for thinking that everything was brand new. Wrong, for the engine Class A3 No. 60102 *Sir Frederick Banbury* first took to the rails in 1922 prior to the grouping, whilst the coaching stock, smart though it may be was built by the LNER before the war. What has actually happened is that the locomotive, allocated to Leicester shed as noted on the bufferbeam, is fresh from a repaint and repair at Doncaster Works in the early blue livery adopted by BR and complete with the lion and wheel emblem on the tender. The coaches were refurbished internally and given the new Maroon and cream colours which became standard on certain regions, then by careful marshalling a complete train was turned out, a sight for sore eyes indeed. The up Master Cutler Express, the morning service from Sheffield to Marylebone has thundered through Arkwright Street and is seen passing the goods warehouse, built by the GCR in 1899 for its London extension. As with its rival on the LMS, this building proclaimed its identity by means of large capital letters in the manner of a frieze just below the top floor windows. Previously, they had spelled out GREAT CENTRAL RAILWAY. The three storey building was adjacent to the down line, rectangular in shape and having hydraulic hoists to the four corners, two of which are prominent in this photograph The cranes working in conjunction with the hoists were capable of serving both internal and outdoor sidings, and although of varying capacity, the maximum weight to be lifted was 1½ tons. the upper two floors comprised storage areas for the great variety of merchandise handled and the top floor had toplights as well as side windows.

All manner of items were received here for despatch, including perhaps gypsum from the Gotham area, beer from the city, textiles and hosiery from many places within the county, cigarettes from John Player & Sons, bicycles from the famous Raleigh factory, soap and other products from Boots, machines and components from the many engineering factories in and around Nottingham, lace making machines from John Jardines whose works were less than half a mile distant in the long vanished Cremorne Street. Quite apart from these, all the more usual items handled by any large goods warehouse could be seen, and for the purpose of lifting very heavy items, such as machines or timber, a 25 ton capacity Goliath crane straddled some of the sidings, this being powered by electricity generated in a small power house within the complex. At ground floor level, three platforms permitted wagons to enter the warehouse, thus being under cover, and public entrances were located in Kirkewhite Street and Wilford Road. In the yard were several small wagon turntables operated by capstan driven by electricity, not horse power. The only inconvenience was the arrangement for serving Clifton Colliery, which was somewhat awkward, necessitating a manoeuvre into the goods yard before reversing onto the branch line which crossed Wilford Road by means of an unguarded level crossing. Latterly this train ran only once each day when the guard had first to clear the highway before the train could pass.

Photo: J.F. Henton

173. Queens Walk. The smug and silver Trent as Shakespeare called it in Henry IV was to have been the boundary between lands controlled by King Henry to the south and those protected by Percy to the north. Taken from the north bank the GCR line, four track at this point, is carried across the river on two adjacent lattice girder bridges set on massive cylindrical piers. The bridge was immediately south of the commodious goods yard known as Queens Walk, and the detail of the brickwork on the approach viaducts is worthy of note. The murky outline of Wilford Power Station may be seen through the nearer bridge arch.

Photo: Author's collection

174. Queens Walk, c.1951. The first signal box to the south of the river was Nottingham Goods South which had under its jurisdiction the connection from the main running lines to the goods lines on the west side. The two bridges were of identical appearance, and the overhead bracing spans show up well taking the outline of a low elipse. The afternoon Manchester–Marylebone express timed to leave Nottingham Victoria at 4.21p.m. is hauled by Class K3 No. 61809. The Woodhead route across the Pennines had not yet been electrified so it was not particularly unusual to find a Gorton engine in charge, as the 39A shedplate proclaims.

Photo: J.F. Henton

175. London Road High Level. This view of London Road High Level Station is taken from the road which gives the station its name and emphasises the purely functional nature of its buildings, overshadowed by a gasometer on one side and the Island Street premises of the Boots Pure Drug Company on the other. An arm of the Nottingham Canal is crossed by the bridge carrying the westerly portion of the station platform and the equally unattractive flat roofed timber buildings of later addition. Many a football fan will have alighted here on Saturday afternoons to walk the short distance to Meadow Lane, the home of Notts County Football Club, and be entertained by the wizardry of Tommy Lawton, undoubtedly their best known player. It was but little further to walk across Trent Bridge where, on the south side of the river, the sporting choice was football at Forest's ground or cricket just across the way, according to season. Football specials for home team supporters found this station to be the most convenient, those originating on ex LNER routes terminating here. The street level buildings still survive, though not in railway use, in the guise of "The Great Central Diner" although the facade has been vastly overtreated with advertising material, which, to say the least, is hard on the eye. *Photo: Author's collection*

176. London Road High Level, 10th March 1965. With the coming of the Great Central Railway at the end of the 19th century, the GNR by contributing half the capital required to build the new station to be known as Victoria, managed at last to secure an excellent position in the city, but not without incurring some considerable expense particularly in the building of this line which connected the two systems, the terminal points being Trent Lane Junction and Weekday Cross Junction between which places it was carried through a predominantly industrial area by a succession of bridges and viaducts. The only station on this short link was the one depicted here at London Road High Level, a dismal and indeed rather ugly place, not at all in keeping with the elegance of the adjacent Low Level premises with which it shares a forecourt. At the beginning of its career its importance was increased for a while, assuming the role of a main line station with through services to London, but on the opening of Victoria being relegated to its intended function as a local station for the benefit of office and factory workers. Empty iron ore tipper wagons retrieved from the Stanton Iron Works near Ilkeston are passing through on the first leg of their return journey to the quarries in east Leicestershire. Mitchells & Butlers Brewery take advantage of the lattice girder bridge spanning London Road to advertise their products, whilst the high ground in the distance is the well known recreation area known as Colwick Woods. *Photo: J.F. Henton*

177. Annesley Shed, 12th May 1956.
As a result of building the locomotive shed at Annesley, the GCR was obliged to make provision for getting men to and from work, because most of them lived several miles away in the Nottingham area. A service was incorporated into the working timetable, though not advertised for public use, running between Bulwell Common and either Hollinwell Halt on the GCR main line or the adjacent Newstead Station on the GNR Leen valley route. This service operated every day of the week at all times of day and night, and was usually entrusted to an engine of some antiquity hauling a couple of coaches which had themselves seen better days. Annesley Shed provided the locomotive, and, for reasons which have never been satisfactorily established, this train came to be called "The Dido". In this view Class C12 No. 67363 passes the GCR style signal box at Annesley North Junction on one of its many daily trips. The pair of tracks to the right form part of the ex-GNR Leen Valley lines whilst on the extreme right of the photograph, by the signals, the station at Hollinwell Halt (previously Hollinwell & Annesley) can just be made out. Although predominantly used by railwaymen, this station was originally meant for use by the golfing fraternity, some of whom can be seen on the course to the left of the signal box roof. *Photo: Author's collection*

178. Annesley Shed, July 1937. When the GCR built its London extension southwards from Annesley to Quainton Road in the dying years of the 19th century it had intended to build a locomotive depot near to Bulwell Common, which would have been convenient, for most of the locomotive department staff lived in that vicinity. However, a great deal of money had been spent in acquiring the land for and building the Victoria Station together with ancillary housing, which meant that the ruling price of land demanded by the owners, especially Nottingham Corporation, was more than the Company was prepared to pay. As a result of this the GCR was compelled to look as far out as Annesley, some ten miles from Victoria, to find a suitable site. This view looking south from the top of the coaling plant shows the six road engine shed lying to the west of the GCR main line, which itself is just out of view. The north light shed had its offices, mess room and stores behind the bay windowed portion and closest to the cinder track which leads from Newstead village, and which may be seen to the right of the sheer legs which stand astride the middle of three outside roads all used for stabling purposes, particularly at weekends. To the right of these a northbound empties train approaches, hauled tender first by a locomotive about to cross the bridge which spans the private driveway leading to Newstead Abbey, and a little further to the right can be seen the GNR signal box which controls the entrance to Newstead Colliery. In the far distance beyond the sidings behind this box is the third line of rails running up the Leen valley, namely the MR Nottingham to Mansfield line. The right of the picture is dominated by the water tower with its associated softening plant, necessary due to the excessive amount of lime found in the "hard" water which rises to the surface in these parts. Immediately to the right of this apparatus lurks the GNR Newstead Station, whilst to the left the row of single storey timber buildings constitutes the GCR barracks at Annesley, reputed to be rat infested, and doubtless very unpopular with visiting enginemen working lodging turns. Being so close to the hustle and bustle of the sheds activities, to say nothing of the noise from Annesley and Newstead Collieries, as well as the GNR line, must have militated strongly against any driver enjoying a rest between shifts. To the left of the two sidings containing locomotive coal stand some redundant locomotive tenders used for removing slurry from the site. The turntable stands unoccupied but ready for use on a day when ex-GCR types are in the majority, although an interesting feature is the Sentinel Steam Railcar which stands on No.1 shed road. The number of private owner wagons on view will also be noted.

Photo: W. Potter